Collins · FLAGSHIP HISTORYMAKERS

HENRY VIII

NICHOLAS FELLOWS

Collins

An imprint of HarperCollins*Publishers*

William Collins' dream of knowledge for all began with the publication of his first book in 1819. A self-educated mill worker, he not only enriched millions of lives, but also founded a flourishing publishing house. Today, staying true to this spirit, Collins books are packed with inspiration, innovation and practical expertise. They place you at the centre of a world of possibility and give you exactly what you need to explore it.

Collins. Do more.

Published by Collins
An imprint of HarperCollins*Publishers*
77–85 Fulham Palace Road
Hammersmith
London
W6 8JB

Browse the complete Collins catalogue at
www.collinseducation.com

© HarperCollins*Publishers* Ltd 2005

10 9 8 7 6 5 4 3 2 1

ISBN 0 00 719986 4

Nicholas Fellows asserts the moral right to be identified as the author of this work.

British Library Cataloguing in Publication Data
A Catalogue record for this publication is available from the British Library

Series commissioned by Graham Bradbury
Project management by Marie Insall
Edited by Sue Chapple
Book design by Derek Lee
Map artwork by Richard Morris
Picture research by Celia Dearing
Production by Sarah Robinson
Printed and bound by Printing Express, Hong Kong

You might also like to visit
www.harpercollins.co.uk
The book lovers' website

ACKNOWLEDGEMENTS
The Publishers would like to thank the following for permission to reproduce pictures on these pages (T = Top, B = Bottom):
T=Top, B=Bottom, L=Left, R=Right, C=Centre

akg images, London, Martin Luther 1528 (oil on wood) studio of Lucas Cranach the Elder 19, akg-images, London/ Erich Lessing, Catherine of Aragon c.1510 (oil on wood) by Michiel Sittow 11TL, Jane Seymour, 1536 (oil on wood) by Hans Holbein the Younger 11BL, Anne of Cleves c.1539 (tempera on canvas) by Hans Holbein the Younger 11TR, Francis I c.1535 (oil on wood) by Jean Clouet 36, Charles V 1533 (oil on canvas) by Titian 20T, akg-images, London / Visioars, Henry VIII meeting with Francis I of France on the Camp du Drap d'Or near Guines in1520, c.1845 (oil on canvas) by Friedrich Bouterwek 38, www.bridgeman.co.uk/Musee Ingres, Montauban, France/Lauros/ Giraudon, The Coronation of Charles V Holy Roman Emperor (oil on canvas) by Cornelius Schut 20B, www.bridgeman.co.uk/ Walker Art Gallery, Henry VIII c.1537 (oil on panel) by Hans Holbein the Younger 7, www.bridgeman.co.uk/Lambeth Palace Library, London, The Great Bible, title page, 1539 17, www.bridgeman.co.uk/ Private Collection 16th century (engraving) English School, Henry VIII and Parliament 55, www.bridgeman.co.uk/ Hever Castle Ltd, Kent, Anne Boleyn 1534 (oil on panel) English School 11CL, www.bridgeman.co.uk/ Lambeth Palace, London, Portrait of a Lady, said to be Katharine Parr 16th century (oil on panel) English School 11BR, www.bridgeman.co.uk/ Ipswich Borough Council Museums and Galleries, Cardinal Wolsey c.16th century (oil on canvas) after Hans Holbein the Younger 33,52, www.bridgeman.co.uk/ Palazzo Barberini Rome, Erasmus of Rotterdam (oil on canvas) by Quentin Massys or Metsys 9T, www.bridgeman.co.uk/ Lambeth Palace, London, Thomas Cranmer painted after 1547 (oil on panel) English School 57, www.bridgeman.co.uk/ The Trustees of Weston Park Foundation, Lord Thomas Cromwell c.16th century, School of Hans Holbein 21,53; Fotomas Index Henry VIII, 1548 (engraving) by Cornelius Metsys 47; National Portrait Gallery, London Edward II and the Pope c.1570 (oil on panel) by an unknown artist 27, Sir Thomas More 1527 (oil on panel) after Hans Holbein the Younger 9B; The Royal Collection © 2004, Her Majesty Queen Elizabeth II, Portrait of a Lady, said to be Catherine Howard 16th century (miniature) by Hans Holbein the Younger 11CR, Henry VIII meeting Maximilian at Battle of the Spurs by an unknown artist 42, Henry VII, Elizabeth of York, Henry VIII and Jane Seymour 1667 by Remigius van Leemput 26.

Cover picture: Portrait of Henry VIII, school of Hans Holbein www.bridgeman.co.uk/ Private Collection/Ackermann and Johnson Ltd, London

Every effort has been made to contact the holders of copyright material, but if any have been inadvertently overlooked the Publishers will be pleased to make the necessary arrangements at the first opportunity.

Contents

Why do historians differ?

THE purpose of the Flagship Historymakers series is to explore the main debates surrounding a number of key individuals in British, European and American History.

Each book begins with a chronology of the significant events in the life of the particular individual, and an outline of the person's career. The book then examines in greater detail three of the most important and controversial issues in the life of the individual – issues which continue to attract differing views from historians, and which feature prominently in examination syllabuses in A level History and beyond.

Each of these issue sections provides students with an overview of the main arguments put forward by historians. By posing key questions, these sections aim to help students to think through the areas of debate and to form their own judgements on the evidence. It is important, therefore, for students to understand why historians differ in their views on past events and, in particular, on the role of individuals in past events.

The study of History is an ongoing debate about events in the past. Although factual evidence is the essential ingredient of history, it is the *interpretation* of factual evidence that forms the basis for historical debate. The study of how and why historians differ in their various interpretations is termed 'historiography'.

Historical debate can occur for a wide variety of reasons:

Insufficient evidence

In some cases there is insufficient evidence to provide a definitive conclusion. In attempting to 'fill the gaps' where factual evidence is unavailable, historians use their professional judgement to make 'informed comments' about the past.

New evidence

As new evidence comes to light, an historian today may have more information on which to base judgements than historians in the past. For instance, a major source of information explaining Philip II's attitude towards the government of Spain was discovered recently in a back street of Madrid, being used as toilet paper! It is only recently that historians have started to assess this evidence and alter their views accordingly.

A 'philosophy' of history?

Many historians have a specific view of history that will affect the way they make their historical judgements. For instance, Marxist historians – who take their view from the writings of Karl Marx, the founder of modern socialism – believe that society has always been made up of competing economic and social classes. They also place considerable importance on economic reasons behind human decision-making. Therefore, a Marxist historian looking at an historical issue may take a completely different viewpoint to a non-Marxist historian.

The role of the individual

Some historians have seen history as being largely moulded by the acts of specific individuals. Henry VIII, Mary Tudor and Elizabeth I are seen as individuals whose personality and beliefs changed the course of sixteenth-century English history. Other historians have tended to play down the roles of individuals; instead, they highlight the importance of more general social, religious, economic and political change. They tend to see the political and religious changes of the sixteenth century as being caused by a broader group of individuals. An example of this might be the emerging gentry class, which was gaining its wealth from the religious changes and began to demand a greater role in government.

Placing different emphasis on the same historical evidence

Even if historians do not possess different philosophies of history or place different emphasis on the role of the individual, it is still possible for them to disagree in one very important way. This is that they may place different emphases on aspects of the same factual evidence. As a result, History should be seen as a subject that encourages debate about the past, based on historical evidence.

Historians will always differ

Historical debate is, in its nature, continuous. What today may be an accepted view about a past event may well change in the future, as the debate continues.

Timeline: Henry VIII's life

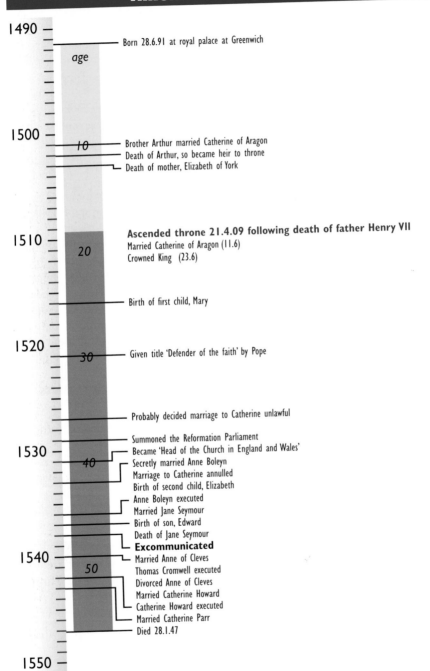

1490	
	Born 28.6.91 at royal palace at Greenwich
	age
1500	
	10 — Brother Arthur married Catherine of Aragon
	Death of Arthur, so became heir to throne
	Death of mother, Elizabeth of York
1510	**Ascended throne 21.4.09 following death of father Henry VII**
	20 Married Catherine of Aragon (11.6)
	Crowned King (23.6)
	Birth of first child, Mary
1520	
	30 Given title 'Defender of the faith' by Pope
	Probably decided marriage to Catherine unlawful
	Summoned the Reformation Parliament
1530	Became 'Head of the Church in England and Wales'
	40 Secretly married Anne Boleyn
	Marriage to Catherine annulled
	Birth of second child, Elizabeth
	Anne Boleyn executed
	Married Jane Seymour
	Birth of son, Edward
	Death of Jane Seymour
	Excommunicated
1540	Married Anne of Cleves
	50 Thomas Cromwell executed
	Divorced Anne of Cleves
	Married Catherine Howard
	Catherine Howard executed
	Married Catherine Parr
	Died 28.1.47
1550	

Henry VIII, painted by Hans Holbein in about 1537, at the height of his power.

Henry VIII: a brief biography

How did he make history?

Henry VIII (1509–1547) is possibly the best known of all English monarchs. Nearly all school children will remember that he had six wives and most will also remember what happened to them through the rhyme 'divorced, beheaded, died, divorced, beheaded, survived'. For others it will be the sheer size of Henry that will be remembered, either the elegant young King of the early years or the fat, bloated tyrant of later years.

However, there was much more to him and the period in which he ruled. It was under Henry that England **broke away from Rome** and established a national Church that would be fully developed under his daughter, Elizabeth. Some historians have argued that it was under Henry that a modern national state was established, with a revolution in government. It is certainly true that Henry had to deal with some of the same problems that face governments today – England's relationship with Europe, for example. He wanted England to become a major power and not be dominated by France, Spain and the **Holy Roman Empire**; even if he did not achieve this, he did lay down the foundations of the modern navy that would allow it to be achieved at a later date.

Broke away from Rome: The process by which Henry ended England's links with the Catholic Church and established a national Church.

Holy Roman Empire: This was largely the land that today makes up Germany and Switzerland. Although the Emperor was elected, the Habsburgs had ruled it since the thirteenth century. The power of the Emperors was very limited.

Henry the man

He was King for just over 37 years, and during this period he changed a great deal. Both his physique and his personality changed. When he came to the throne he was tall, attractive, muscular and well proportioned; when he died he was fat, bloated, nearly blind and had to be moved by a series of hoists. He repulsed most that saw him.

His interests also changed. At the start of his reign he was a keen sportsman who loved hunting, jousting and tennis. By the end of his reign he was reduced to falconry, the Tudor equivalent of the elderly playing bowls! Despite his sporting interests, Henry was also highly cultured. He was a fair musician, if the works attributed to him were actually his, and a reasonably accomplished theological scholar, ironically given the title 'Defender of the Faith' by the Pope in recognition of his work attacking Martin Luther (see page 19).

However, it was in his attitudes to others that the most noticeable change occurred. As he grew older his temper grew worse and it became more dangerous, even life-threatening, to disagree with him.

The happy family man of the early years, secure in his marriage, became the insecure tyrant willing to believe accusations against his wives and advisors.

His early life

Henry was born in 1491 at the royal palace of Greenwich. He was the third child of Henry VII's marriage to Elizabeth of York, but more importantly he was the second son and therefore not heir to the throne. As a result, until he was 11 he was brought up with his sisters at Eltham Palace, largely under the control of his mother. It was a happy, united family. There was no doubt that Henry was a bright child, particularly adept at languages and, surprisingly for a small boy, he loved history. As the only male in a female household he dominated the scene and as a result gained enormous confidence. Even as a child he cut a dashing and regal figure; **Erasmus** commented upon this when he visited Eltham and it was seen by all at his brother Arthur's wedding in 1501 when he threw off his robes and danced at the festivities.

However, Henry's world changed in the space of a few months in 1502–3. First, his brother Arthur died, which meant that Henry was now heir to the throne. Then his mother, only 38, died. Henry was still just 12 and he had lost the person to whom he was closest. Furthermore, he now had to be brought up as the future King and to be protected as the only male Tudor.

The early years as King

Henry VII died on 21 April 1509. On 11 June, the young Henry married his dead brother's wife, **Catherine of Aragon**, then on 23 June was crowned Henry VIII. He was nearly 18 years old and presented a complete contrast to his father. Henry VII was considered mean, was rarely seen in public and was feared by many because of the heavy penalties he exacted from wrong-doers. As a result, Henry's accession was greeted with joy and contemporaries commented on the change of mood that pervaded the country. **Thomas More** stated that 'This day is the end of our slavery, the fount of our liberty; the end of sadness and the beginning of joy'.

This view was quickly reflected in action. Henry was determined to show that he was very different to his father. He soon cast away many of his father's advisors and policies; the first to go were the hated tax collectors Empson and Dudley, a sure way

Desiderius Erasmus (?1469–1536)
A well-known and respected European scholar. He translated the Bible and had a great impact in England where he inspired a group of scholars known as humanists, who wanted a simple religion based on an accurate translation of the Bible. For a time, Erasmus was Professor of Divinity at Cambridge University. He was a critic of the Church, attacking relics, rituals and the structure of monastic life.

Thomas More (1478–1535)
One of Europe's leading humanist scholars and the author of *Utopia*. He was also a royal servant and was appointed Lord Chancellor in 1529, but resigned over Henry's divorce. Although a very close friend of the King, he was executed in 1535.

to gain popularity! Henry was also keen to pursue the kingly activity of war and this followed in 1512–13 with war against both France and Scotland. The gains in France were minimal (see page 34), but his actions did put him firmly at the centre of European politics. Victory over the Scots (although achieved whilst Henry was campaigning in France) was significant in its own right, as it removed the Scottish threat for some decades. It appeared as if the reign had started in a blaze of glory.

However, it soon became apparent that Henry was bored by the everyday work of reading state papers and this paved the way for the rise of his first great minister, Thomas Wolsey. Wolsey had already proved himself a capable administrator in the difficult task of organising supplies for the campaign in France, and his willingness to carry out the daily routine of government ensured his rapid promotion. Some historians have even suggested that Wolsey came to dominate policy-making.

The King's 'great matter'

Although Henry had been happily married to Catherine of Aragon for many years, the marriage had produced only one living child, and that was a girl, Mary Tudor. Henry was desperate for a son, and believed that the failure to have one was a sign from God that his marriage was illegal (since Catherine was his brother's widow). And as Catherine grew older, the chances of any more children were receding.

By the mid 1520s, however, Henry had met and fallen deeply in love with **Anne Boleyn**. Anne refused to accept Henry's sexual advances until she was sure they would be married, and even if she had agreed, any child born outside marriage would have had a dubious claim to the throne. A divorce from Catherine became vital, so that Henry could marry Anne. Pressure on the Pope to grant a divorce proved unsuccessful, and the only way for Henry to solve his problem was to break with Rome. Wolsey's failure to obtain the divorce led to his fall from power, whilst the news that Anne was now pregnant made a solution even more urgent.

Act in Restraint of Appeals 1533: This prevented English people appealing to the Pope over religious matters. The highest court was now in England. It meant that Catherine could not appeal to the Pope over the divorce.

Henry was forced into taking drastic action. The Archbishop of Canterbury Thomas Cranmer declared Henry's divorce and Parliament, led by Henry's new chief minister Thomas Cromwell, passed the **Act in Restraint of Appeals** in 1533. This prevented Catherine from appealing to the Pope to alter the verdict. Henry was now supreme in England and the Act of Supremacy in 1534 confirmed Henry as head of the Church in England. The Act of

Henry VIII's wives

1
Catherine of Aragon (1485–1536)

The daughter of Ferdinand of Aragon and Isabella of Castile. She married Henry VII's eldest son, Arthur, as part of the King's policy to secure the Tudor dynasty. When Arthur died, she remained in England and was betrothed to Henry, who married her in 1509.

4
Anne of Cleves (1515–??)

Married to Henry as part of his attempts to build an alliance against a possible Catholic invasion. Henry had been enchanted by the painting of her, but was disgusted when he first saw her and only went ahead with the marriage out of diplomatic necessity. Once the threat of invasion had gone he divorced her.

2
Anne Boleyn (?1501–1536)

The daughter of Sir Thomas Boleyn and related to the Norfolk family, she was sent to France when 12, but upon return joined the royal court. Her sister was already the King's mistress, but Henry soon fell madly in love with Anne. At first, she refused to be his mistress and this led, in part, to the divorce from Catherine. She was the mother of Elizabeth, but was executed in 1536 for adultery.

5
Catherine Howard (?1520–1542)

The niece of the Catholic Duke of Norfolk, who was the leader of the conservative faction. Henry married her in 1540. She was executed for adultery.

3
Jane Seymour (1509–1537)

Reputedly Henry's favourite wife, he married her in 1536 and she gave the King the longed-for male heir, Edward.

6
Catherine Parr (1512–1548)

Henry's last wife, well educated and a supporter of humanist and reformist ideas. She married Henry in 1543.

Succession ended any claim that Catherine might have to be Henry's lawful wife and declared their daughter Mary illegitimate. In order to achieve his divorce, Henry had been forced to abandon his links with Rome and establish a national Church. However, it is apparent from the lack of doctrinal changes that followed the break that Henry was more concerned with gaining power over the Church and using its wealth for his own ends. This was confirmed by the Dissolution of the Monasteries in the 1530s (see page 24), which gave the King large sums of money with which to improve England's defences and reward those who had supported his break with Rome.

The peak of power?

Henry was now supreme in his own realm, yet still he was not secure. The divorce and subsequent religious changes were unpopular with many. Anne was subject to frequent abuse and referred to as a whore, whilst the closure of the monasteries prompted the largest Tudor rebellion, the Pilgrimage of Grace (see page 50). The money he had raised from the Dissolution had to be used to strengthen defences against a possible Catholic crusade from France and Spain. Just as importantly, the marriage to Anne failed to bring the much-needed male heir; instead, another girl, Elizabeth, was born. Anne's failure to produce a son meant that she was soon cast aside, and subsequently executed, following trumped-up charges of incest and adultery. At the same time, Elizabeth was declared illegitimate and lost her place in the succession.

However, it did seem that Henry had found contentment with his third wife, **Jane Seymour**. She was able to provide the male heir, Edward, that Henry so desired. Unfortunately, his joy was short-lived as the birth resulted in complications and Jane died in October 1537. Henry was sincere in his mourning but was soon looking for another wife. The need for allies in Europe against a possible Catholic invasion following his excommunication by the Pope in 1538, led him to marry the German Anne of Cleves. Encouraged by Cromwell and the painting he had seen of her, Henry was convinced she would be acceptable. However, as soon as he saw her he was displeased, declaring that she was 'nothing as well as she was spoken of'. As soon as the political situation improved, Henry determined to get rid of both her and the advisor, Cromwell, who had taken him into the marriage. This became even more desirable once he had been introduced to the attractive young **Catherine Howard**, niece of one of Cromwell's opponents, the Duke of Norfolk.

The last years

Henry's last years were characterised by factional struggle. Although one of the reasons for Cromwell's fall was the disastrous Cleves marriage, **faction** and religion also played a key role. The Howards realised that they could use Catherine to bring down Cromwell, gain power in government and so prevent any further moves towards Protestantism. They appeared to have achieved their goal in 1540 when Cromwell was arrested and executed.

The fall of Cromwell did not end the factional struggles but rather intensified them, as Henry decided against appointing a new chief minister. The 1540s would therefore see a struggle between the religiously conservative ministers, who initially appeared to be on top with the passing of the **Act of Six Articles**, and the reformers. Then the conservatives started to lose their ascendancy. Henry was besotted with Catherine Howard but the age difference meant that she soon had other admirers at court and in 1541 Henry was presented with evidence that she had committed adultery. Catherine was beheaded, along with those implicated in the affair. Worse was to follow for the conservatives when they tried to drive a wedge between the King and Archbishop Cranmer, accusing Cranmer of Protestant heresy. Henry rejected the charge and went on to marry **Catherine Parr**. This made a significant change to the balance at court as she was related to the Seymours and was a known Protestant sympathiser. The court soon saw the presence of Protestant scholars and the education of Edward and Elizabeth was in the hands of Protestant tutors. The Catholic faction tried to hit back by accusing members of Catherine Parr's household of heresy but the King stood by his Queen.

By the end of Henry's reign, the Protestant faction was dominant. As Henry's health declined, he spent more time in his private apartments and the role of Chief Gentleman of King's Privy Chamber, Sir Anthony Denny (a reformer), became crucial as he controlled access to the King. The Catholic faction lost further influence with the arrests of Norfolk and his son, the Earl of Surrey, who was executed a week before Henry died. The other leading Catholic councillor, Stephen Gardiner, was excluded from the Regency Council. Henry's will was firmly in the hands of the reform faction.

Henry died on 27 January 1547, but news of his death was kept quiet by the reform faction for three days to allow them the chance to gain possession of Henry's son Edward. They had already altered Henry's will, strengthening their own position, and now proceeded to appoint Seymour as Lord Protector, ensuring the triumph and domination of the reform faction in the new regime.

Faction: A group of people who have got together for a common political purpose, usually to advance their cause or to stop others. In the 1540s, it was often also associated with religion. The key factions at Henry's court in the 1540s were groups led by the conservative Howards (Catholic) and the reforming Seymours (Protestant).

Act of Six Articles 1539: These articles reversed many of the Protestant ideas of the Ten Articles of 1536. They upheld Catholic beliefs such as transubstantiation, and attacked the Protestant belief in clerical marriage.

Understanding Henry VIII

- **An intelligent and well-educated man**, who had a love of history and had impressed Erasmus and More at a young age. He spoke French, Latin and a little Italian.

- **A dominant monarch**, who was determined to get his way. Although he was not always interested in day-to-day government, he could get heavily involved and dominate decision-making.

- **A man with great charm, but also a temper**, and even a streak of cruelty, who could turn on his friends as well as his enemies. It is alleged that he hit Thomas Cromwell.

- **He wanted to be an Imperial King**. This placed the King next to God in importance. Henry had this stated in the Act in Restraint of Appeals and also used the imperial crown as a motif.

- **Eager to conquer**, he spent vast sums of money in wars against France and Scotland.

- **A man who could not be trusted.** He was not loyal to his two greatest servants, Thomas Wolsey and Thomas Cromwell, and he had his closest friend, Thomas More, executed. He also got rid of his wives when they failed him.

- **A rash man**, he did not see the longer-term consequences of his actions, but was more concerned with satisfying his immediate pleasure.

- **A formidable man**, he was not only physically large, but also had great presence.

- **A religiously complex man**, but ultimately conservative in his beliefs.

- **An egotistical monarch** who wanted to be remembered as a warrior king, like Henry V, and as being greater than his father.

> *'A vivid and active mind, above measure able to execute whatever tasks he undertook .... You would say he was a universal genius.'*
> Erasmus

How Protestant was England?

What were Henry's religious beliefs?

Why did Henry break with Rome?

What factors influenced religious changes 1536–1547?

Framework of Events

1521	Henry given title 'Defender of the Faith' by the Pope
1526–7	Henry decides on a divorce from Catherine
1527	Charles V sacks Rome
1529	Proceedings for the divorce start to be heard
	Reformation Parliament is called
1532	Anne Boleyn becomes pregnant
1533	Act in Restraint of Appeals, which prevents Catherine taking her case to Rome
	Cranmer rules that Henry's marriage to Catherine is invalid
	Henry marries Anne
1534	Act of Supremacy
1536	Act for the Dissolution of the Smaller Monasteries
	Ten Articles
1539	Six Articles and Publication of the Bible in English
1540	Cromwell arrested and executed
1543	King's Book
1547	Regency Council established, containing many with Reformist sympathies

What were Henry's religious beliefs?

Historians have interpreted Henry's religious beliefs in a great variety of ways, ranging from: 'Catholicism without the Pope' or 'National Catholicism'; through a middle way, balancing Catholicism with the new reformed religion; to a conservative form of Protestantism. Other interpretations have suggested that Henry's religious beliefs were either those of convenience or that politics came before religion. All of these interpretations have at least some justification, but in order to understand events after 1529 it is important to try and understand what Henry might have truly believed, as he played a major role in the development and direction of religious policy.

'National Catholicism'

At the start of Henry's reign England was part of the Catholic Church; it owed allegiance to the Pope and followed traditional Catholic practices. Henry himself was a good amateur theologian. His own Bible is full of annotations and comments, suggesting that he read it carefully. Most memorably, he had written a book in defence of Catholicism and the Papacy when they were attacked by Martin Luther, and in recognition had received the title 'Defender of the Faith' from the Pope. Historians agree that these were his genuine views and were not simply written for the political gain that resulted.

A middle way

Those historians who argue that Henry's views reflected a middle way, support their argument by showing that the Henrician Church on the one hand rejected purgatory, yet retained prayers for the dead; and accepted images, yet rejected their veneration. Perhaps the clearest indication of a middle way was the execution in 1540 of three Catholics for affirming papal supremacy and the burning, on virtually the same day, of three Protestants for upholding the Lutheran belief of justification by faith. Henry's policy was perhaps best summarised by Diarmaid MacCulloch, who described it as 'a ragbag of emotional preferences'.

A very conservative Protestantism

Another basis for Henry's approach to religion was suggested by Pamela Tudor-Craig in *Henry VIII and King David* (1989), in which she argued that Henry identified himself with the Old Testament King David. Other historians have developed this view and suggested that a model of Old Testament kingship is, in fact, crucial in understanding Henry's position after he became Supreme Head of the Church in 1534. This interpretation adopts the same view as the propaganda of the 1530s. These works suggested that it was the duty of the King to discipline ministers and bishops and to ensure

Frontispiece of the English Bible, showing Henry at the centre carrying out his duty of spreading the Christian word.

that they carried out their duties in a conscientious manner. Even a conservative bishop wrote in 1539 that Henry had acted as 'the chief and best of the kings of Israel did, and as all good Christian kings ought to do'. According to this interpretation the King had God-given authority over the church. Once Henry had realised that this was his role, it was his duty to carry it out. It was also possible to argue that in the past he had been deceived about the extent of his power by the papacy, which had intruded into areas that belonged to the King. Therefore, all that Henry was doing was regaining lost power. This was certainly the view that Henry and his chief minister, Thomas Cromwell, wanted to portray in the 1530s, as they argued that the changes were conservative and that Henry was simply taking back powers that used to be the King's.

There is certainly an argument that suggests Henry saw religious developments in terms of politics. Henry was prepared to allow the **Bible** to be published **in English** because it was partly used to teach people their obligations. According to priests and propagandists the obligation of the people to the King was obedience. Therefore religion was used as a prop to uphold the Tudor regime and, at a time when there was no police force to enforce discipline, it was a useful method.

It is also possible to argue, as Margaret Aston has shown in *England's Iconoclasts* (1989), that Old Testament kings were associated with the destruction of idolatry and that these ideas were at least considered by Henry. This interpretation is supported by the **investigation into the monasteries** in 1535 and the destruction of images in 1538. Even in the 1540s, when historians have identified a conservative reaction, the King never retreated from his earlier position and several shrines were pulled down.

Bible in English: The Great Bible was published in English in 1539. All parish churches were ordered to buy a copy. Some historians believe that this had a great impact in ensuring that England became Protestant, as it made the Bible accessible to all.

Investigation into the monasteries: In 1535 Cromwell sent a team around the country to investigate the condition of the monasteries. The team was instructed to find any information that would show the monasteries in a poor light, in order to justify their closure.

Why did Henry VIII break with Rome?

Two schools of thought

There are two schools of thought concerning Henry's decision to break with Rome. The first, usually called the traditionalist, has argued that the Church in England was suffering from a variety of abuses and a lack of spirituality. As a consequence there was a general feeling of **anti-clericalism** among ordinary people, which put pressure on the King to reform the Church. This view, put forward by historians such as A. G. Dickens in *The English Reformation* (1964), has argued that even without Henry's desire for a divorce from his first wife, there would have been some form of **Reformation**. Dickens argued that the criticism of the Church had 'created before the meeting of the Reformation Parliament an atmosphere little short of explosive'. He suggested that the move towards Protestantism was driven by a popular dislike for the Catholic Church, arguing that 'the majority of people cannot possibly have been ardent or even convinced Catholics'.

This view remained the accepted orthodoxy until the late 1980s, when it was challenged by historians such as Christopher Haigh. In *The English Reformation Revised* (1987) Haigh argued that 'The English people had not turned against their Church, and there was no widespread yearning for reform.' This view was supported by Eamon Duffy in *The Stripping of the Altars* (1992), where he argued that 'Late medieval Catholicism exerted an enormously strong, diverse and vigorous hold over the imagination and loyalty of the people up to the very moment of the Reformation'.

These historians, usually called **revisionists**, have argued that the Catholic Church was thriving on the eve of the Reformation and that Catholicism was popular until the 1580s in some parts of the country. This led Haigh to search for other reasons for the break with Rome – and he found the answer in the political developments of the period and Henry's need for a divorce from Catherine.

Most historians would now agree that the divorce played a vital role in the Reformation, by causing Henry to question who should control the English Church. This questioning was the result of Henry's denial of the Pope's right to issue a dispensation over Catherine's marriage to his brother Arthur. However, it must also be remembered that Henry went to great lengths to persuade the Pope to grant a divorce, suggesting that he was not completely against papal authority. This also supports the argument that the break

Anti-clericalism: A general term used to describe opposition to the Church, but this opposition had many opinions and views.

Reformation: A term used to describe the religious changes that took place between 1529 and 1603. Although at a legal level the changes were largely complete by 1559, it was not until much later that many parishes became Protestant.

Revisionist: the term applied to historians who have challenged the traditional interpretation of events.

with Rome and subsequent Reformation was undertaken with reluctance.

The legitimacy of Henry's marriage

Henry had been married to Catherine since 1509 and to suddenly start questioning the validity of this marriage does, at first sight, suggest that Henry was desperately looking for excuses to end it. Furthermore, he had by the mid-1520s fallen in love with the young and attractive Anne Boleyn. This is revealed by a series of love letters written to her by Henry, usually a reluctant writer, and is the interpretation of Peter Gwyn, in *The King's Cardinal: The Rise and Fall of Thomas Wolsey* (1990) where he argues that 'the one argument for the divorce that Henry never made in public was that he had fallen in love with Anne, for to have done so would have been tactically foolish.' However, Anne was very astute and refused to become Henry's mistress until she was secure in the knowledge that she would become Queen. Henry's desire to end his marriage was further encouraged by the fact that Catherine had become too old to have children.

Defender of the Faith: The title given to Henry by the Pope, for his book attacking Martin Luther. It is still used by British monarchs today.

Although there is certainly some truth in this view, as Starkey has made clear in *Six Wives* (2003), it has also been shown that Henry was a very religious man. His bible is full of annotations and he had already gained the title **Defender of the Faith** for his attack on **Martin Luther**. Therefore, it is possible that Henry genuinely believed that it was unlawful for him to marry his dead brother's wife, particularly if the marriage had been consummated, and that no Pope could issue a dispensation for this. Henry may also have genuinely believed that the lack of a son from this 'marriage' was God's punishment. This view is supported by Eric Ives, in *Anne Boleyn* (1986), where he argues that 'Henry had no option as a devout Christian but to obey, to contract a legal marriage and a son would be the reward'.

Martin Luther (1483–1546)
A German, Roman Catholic monk who published his 95 theses attacking Catholic beliefs in 1517. These were intended for scholarly debate, but the ideas soon spread and were the trigger for the Reformation.

The legitimacy of Mary Tudor

If Henry's marriage to Catherine was illegal it meant that their daughter, Mary Tudor, was illegitimate. Indeed, a number of factors led Henry to question her suitability to be heir to the throne, not least whether a female could inherit the throne. Even if she could, there were fears that it would result in unrest and instability. There were also descendants of Edward IV who were alive and might lay claim to the throne and undo the Tudor achievement. The issue of Mary's legitimacy had also

**Charles V
(1500–1558):** The uncle of Catherine of Aragon, Charles was the ruler of Spain and the Netherlands from 1516–56. In 1519, he was elected Holy Roman Emperor, which meant he was the most powerful ruler in Europe.

The coronation of Charles V, Holy Roman Emperor, by the Pope.

been raised during Henry and Anne's visit to France in 1528 to try and secure a French alliance, when negotiations had taken place over the possible marriage of Mary to the French heir to the throne. There is no doubt that Henry was concerned about Mary's suitability to rule as he made moves to legitimise his bastard son, the Duke of Richmond, and also to give him experience of government as he was sent to run the Council of the North.

Foreign policy

When Henry had married Catherine the marriage had political value in strengthening the alliance with Spain, but that Spanish alliance was now diminishing in importance. Spain had at times proved an unreliable ally and it no longer seemed as vital to have the aunt of the Emperor as your wife. Henry also hoped that military pressure could be used to force **Charles V** to agree to the divorce (see page 40). In order to achieve this, England and France had declared war in 1528 against Charles. Henry wanted to ensure that the alliance with France survived and the best way to achieve this was through a marriage treaty, but the doubts over the legitimacy of Mary were a stumbling block. However, although the war started well for France this did not last. In 1529, a

crucial victory for Charles against Francis and the subsequent Peace of Cambrai meant that any hope Henry had of forcing the Habsburgs to agree to a divorce through military pressure were ended. As a result Charles still controlled the Pope and was able to prevent him from agreeing to Henry's request for a divorce.

Power

Although Henry is often depicted as having a powerful ego, wanting to be supreme, historians have disagreed about how far this motivated his decision to break with Rome. The break did make the King in Parliament supreme over all matters relating to the Church, including doctrine and organisation, but how far this was Henry's aim at the outset is debatable.

A. F. Pollard in *Henry VIII* (1902) argued that Henry wanted to be all-powerful. In his interpretation, Henry was determined to exercise supreme power in England and therefore 'the divorce, in fact, was the occasion and not the cause of the Reformation'. The Church's refusal to allow the divorce gave Henry the ideal opportunity to rid himself of the power of the Church and to be his own master. According to Pollard this was encouraged by a growing sense of nationalism within the country, which was voiced in Parliament.

The Act in Restraint of Appeals had made Henry supreme head of the Church in England. This was reinforced by the Act of Supremacy, which declared that Henry 'rightfully is Supreme Head of the Church of England'. However, the events prior to the break with Rome suggest that an increase in royal power was not the motivating factor for Henry. The King spent a long time trying to persuade the Pope to grant the divorce, suggesting that he was never completely against papal authority. This is reinforced by events after the initial attack, as the First **Act of Annates** was conditional, giving the Pope the chance to nullify the marriage and supporting the view that Henry would have abandoned the break.

Although power may not have been the main driving force behind Henry's decisions, Elton in *The Tudor Revolution in Government* (1953) has argued that it was not Henry but **Thomas Cromwell** who was the real architect of the break. He argues that it was Cromwell who drafted the Act in Restraint of Appeals and offered 'to make a reality out of Henry's vague claims to supremacy'. In Elton's version of events Cromwell was politically motivated, he wanted to 'reconstruct the body

Act of Annates: Annates were the payment of the first year's salary of a bishop to Rome; this Act stopped the payment. The first act would only come into force in a year's time, but if Henry was given his divorce it would be dropped. Henry was using it to put pressure on the Pope to agree to the divorce.

Thomas Cromwell (1485?–1540)
He rose from a humble background to become a lawyer. He worked for Wolsey but survived his fall, becoming a Privy councillor in 1531 and secretary to the King in 1534. He was the Henry's principal minister from 1532 to his fall in 1540. His fall was largely the result of the disastrous Cleves marriage and the faction struggle between the religious conservatives and reformists.

politic', in which King and Parliament would act together. However, Elton's view that it was effectively a revolution is no longer accepted by many historians.

Money

There is no doubt that on the eve of the Reformation the Church was a rich institution. Simon Fish in his 'Supplication for the Beggars', written in 1529, argued that the Church owned one third of the wealth of the land. Although this was a piece of propaganda designed to discredit the Church, Henry would have been aware of the considerable amount of wealth that a break from Rome would release for him. The early acts of the Reformation Parliament, such as the charge of **Praemunire** in 1530–1, show that the King saw how he could obtain money that had previously been heading to Rome.

Praemunire: A Latin term, which made it a crime to use powers or laws derived from the Pope in England.

However, to argue that money was the main cause of the break is difficult to sustain. Cromwell may have promised to make Henry 'the richest man in Christendom', but once again a study of the chronology of events suggests that the acquisition of Church wealth was a bonus. The Dissolution of the Monasteries did not start immediately following the break. It was gradual – the closure of small houses in 1536 brought little financial gain and the dissolution of the larger houses did not occur until the foreign situation meant that Henry was in urgent need of money in order to fortify the south coast against a possible Catholic crusade.

Religion and doctrine

A study of the legislation passed by the Reformation Parliament makes it very clear that doctrinal change played virtually no part in the decision to break with Rome. The early changes were largely jurisdictional, giving Henry legal power over the Church. It can be argued that it was not until the dissolution of the smaller monasteries in 1536 that the first signs of doctrinal change were witnessed, as their closure could be seen as a challenge to the doctrine of purgatory. However, two points do need to be stressed. Firstly doctrinal change did not come about until Thomas Cromwell, a supporter of the reformed religion, was firmly in charge. This interpretation is supported by D. MacCulloch, in *Thomas Cranmer* (1996), who argues that 'the woeful number of loose ends in the Supremacy, exposed by the events of 1534, led to a stage-by-stage rethink, which in the end would leave the Archbishop [Cranmer] much more clearly the junior partner to the vice-regent in spiritual [Cromwell].' The second point is that at the first sign of doctrinal change there was widespread opposition, the Pilgrimage of Grace (see page 50). There had been very limited resistance to the break previously, because most of the population would have noticed little change. The Reformation only really became noticeable with the loss of the monasteries that provided ordinary people with support in times of need and a place of worship and religious teaching.

Although a number of factors influenced the break with Rome, it seems reasonable to suggest that it was largely a political process. This would explain why it was Cromwell, rather than Cranmer, who was the driving force behind the legislation. However, it is also important to remember that ultimately it was Henry who made the decisions. Most recent research suggests that Henry genuinely believed that his marriage to Catherine was unlawful, for as Peter Gwyn argues in *The King's Cardinal: The Rise and Fall of Thomas Wolsey*, 'it is difficult to see how Henry could have sustained the campaign for the five and a half years that were needed, or that he would have jeopardised so much in order to do so' unless he was convinced of his cause.

What factors influenced religious changes 1536–1547?

Four phases of change

The religious changes of this period can to a certain extent be divided into four phases. The first phase saw a swing towards the reformed, or Protestant, faith, and was characterised by the start of the Dissolution of the Monasteries in 1536, as well as the Act of Ten Articles and **Royal Injunctions**. It appeared to come to an end in the period 1538–9 with the Act of Six Articles, although this is a very simplistic view as the larger monasteries were not dissolved until after the Act of Six Articles.

The second phase is usually characterised by a return to more traditional Catholic practices and appeared to start with the trial and execution of John Lambert for rejecting **transubstantiation**. It reached a climax with the removal of Cromwell, and Henry's marriage to Catherine Howard, in 1540. The third phase is best described as one of confusion. This is perhaps best characterised by the **King's Book**, which defended the Catholic belief of transubstantiation, but also encouraged preaching and attacked images. The final phase, in Henry's last year, witnessed the triumph of the reform faction. Henry appointed a heavily Protestant Regency

Royal Injunctions: Instructions issued to the clergy by Cromwell in 1536 and 1538. They were used to promote the reformed religion.

Transubstantiation: The belief that during Mass the bread and wine are transformed into the body and blood of Christ.

King's Book, 1543: Also known as 'The Necessary Doctrine and Erudition of a Christian Man', it upheld Catholic beliefs.

Council for Edward and this ensured the ultimate triumph of the reformed faith in the next reign.

Why were the monasteries dissolved?

The Dissolution of the Monasteries occurred in two phases; the smaller houses, those with an income of under £200 per year, were dissolved in 1536, whilst the larger houses were closed in 1539–40. It is likely that different factors were important at different times. It is also important to remember that dissolution was not a new idea; Wolsey had closed 29 monasteries in the 1520s.

Henry and Cromwell had different motives for the closure. Foremost in Henry's mind was the need for the money that could be gained by the closure of the larger monasteries; many had net incomes of over £1000 per year. This was particularly important when there was a genuine fear of a Catholic crusade following Henry's excommunication in 1538. At the same time the money would reduce the need for taxation – always a popular move and one that might influence those who were otherwise opposed to the religious changes. As A. G. Dickens has argued, it would endow the crown in perpetuity and help to achieve political stability.

The closures also offered Henry the opportunity of land which could be sold, used as patronage or given as a reward for loyalty. There is certainly evidence that Henry used the land to reward those who supported the religious changes of the period, and even Catholics such as the Duke of Norfolk were willing to cash in on this bonanza, putting their greed before religious conviction. Therefore Henry was able to use the land to buy off potential opposition.

Although Cromwell certainly saw the financial benefits that the Crown would gain from the Dissolution, it is likely that he himself had other motives. He was a supporter of the reformed faith and probably saw the monasteries as a bastion of the old Catholic faith, which needed to be removed if the true religion was to be established. He would already have seen that religious houses had been closed in Germany and areas of Scandinavia where the Reformation had taken hold. This may explain why he was anxious to show how corrupt the monasteries were, and why those who were sent out to survey them were given instructions to find and publicise any bad behaviour they found.

The role of Thomas Cromwell

One of the charges brought against Cromwell when he fell from power in 1540 was that he was a Lutheran. His position as

Vice-Regent: The Act of Supremacy had given Henry the power to put a layman in charge of religious affairs. This meant that Cromwell had more power than Wolsey over the Church.

Vice-Regent in charge of religious affairs meant that his was the greatest day-to-day influence on religious policy in the period 1536–1540 and it is therefore likely that he played a significant role in the moves towards Protestantism. There are certainly instances when his religious views appear to have influenced policy. He put pressure on the bishops to secure their agreement to the publication and national distribution of a Bible in English in 1539. He also issued detailed Injunctions in 1536 and 1538 to ensure that Catholic practices such as pilgrimages were discouraged, and relics removed from churches. These Injunctions were reinforced by letters to JPs ordering them to check that the bishops were following the instructions. He was therefore able to ensure that decisions made in central government were imposed in the localities.

The greatest period of Cromwell's influence was probably 1537–8. Two significant moves towards Protestantism were achieved in this period. The first was the Bishop's Book, written by senior members of the clergy, which failed to uphold many Catholic practices such as transubstantiation. It also downplayed other Catholic beliefs, such as mass, the special status of priests and purgatory. This was certainly Cromwell's work, as Henry was too busy to read the book and insisted that the work was not published in his name until he had read it. The second important step was the ordering of an English Bible to be placed in every parish within two years, which must be available for parishioners to read. Cromwell himself took on the responsibility for ensuring that this target was achieved. It meant that the whole population was able to find out what the Bible actually said and, according to some Protestant historians, this ensured the ultimate triumph of Protestantism.

The role of Henry

The traditional view of Henry is that he was a religious conservative who tried to prevent any changes in the doctrine of the Church following the break with Rome. This argument is supported by the events of 1539–1543, which featured a return to more traditional practices as seen in the Act of Six Articles of 1539 or the **Act for the Advancement of True Religion.** This view was challenged by J. Scarisbrick in his biography of Henry VIII in 1968, where he argued that the interpretation was too simplistic; it is still possible to suggest that Henry did possess certain religious prejudices which influenced policy.

Act for the Advancement of True Religion: This Act limited those who were allowed to read the Bible. Only upper class men and noble women, in private, were allowed this privilege. It denied access to the lower orders as it was feared how they would interpret and use it.

However, it must also be remembered that Henry used religion as a political instrument. He was, for example, prepared to consider

Henrvy VIII with his father. The inscription proclaims that, although Henry VII was great, Henry VIII was greater as he brought the Church under royal control.

further moves towards Protestantism in order to obtain an alliance with the German princes when security of the realm was at stake. He had also supported the Dissolution of the Monasteries and would have allowed the **Dissolution of the Chantries** had he lived longer, despite supporting all that they stood for.

Dissolution of the Chantries: Chantries were small chapels whose main purpose was for saying prayers for the souls of the dead. The Act closing them was not enforced until after Henry died.

At the same time, Henry saw that religion could be divisive and it is possible to argue that the policy adopted in England was a pragmatic response. Henry did not want to see his kingdom wracked by a civil war caused by religious extremism and therefore, until the very end of his reign, ensured that there was a religious balance within the country. This would explain the decision to execute groups of both Protestants and Catholics in 1540. It would also help to explain his decision to limit access to the Bible in 1543.

There is no doubt that Henry had a considerable influence over policy, particularly after the removal of Cromwell. It can even be suggested that one of the reasons for the removal of the advisor was that his religious policy was becoming too extreme for Henry and appeared to be threatening order. Henry certainly directed policy throughout much of the later years.

Henry VIII's deathbed. The Pope is shown crushed and Henry is pointing to Edward as his successor.

To what extent did foreign policy influence religious policy?

Although Henry was generally cautious and conservative in his approach to religious policy, it is possible to argue that his need for an alliance with the German Protestant princes against Charles V, in 1537–8, encouraged moves towards Protestantism. The period 1539–43 then witnessed a swing back towards Catholicism and some historians have argued that the passing of the Act of Six Articles in June 1539 was intended to demonstrate to Europe that a campaign against England was unjustified on religious grounds. However, it has also been argued that its passing was due less to the fear of invasion than concern for order at home. This argument suggests that foreign policy was less significant in influencing religious policy than was once thought.

Conclusion

Some historians have argued that fundamentally England was still a Catholic country upon the death of Henry. Even if this were true, certain changes – such as the Dissolution of the Monasteries – meant that it would subsequently be very difficult to restore a full Roman Catholic Church. However, some historians have gone further and suggested that events in Henry's reign (the introduction of the English Bible, the appointment of people such as Cranmer, and the attack on relics and pilgrimages, for example) would ensure the ultimate triumph of Protestantism.

   It is very difficult to ascertain the actual religious situation in the country. Events at court were confused as different factions were dominant (see Chapter 3, pages 56–59) and there were moves to both further and halt Protestantism during the last few years of the reign. Meanwhile, in the countryside as a whole, work by Duffy and Haigh would suggest that most of the population were still Catholic. This interpretation is supported by Susan Brigden's study of London, *London and the Reformation* (1989), which argued that only 20% of the population were Protestant. There were some substantial minorities in other parts of the south-east and East Anglia, but in most other areas Protestantism was virtually non-existent. However, this view was challenged by Robert Whiting in *The Blind Devotion of the People* (1989), where he suggested that expenditure on Church goods declined after 1540, showing a loss of support for the established Church. This interpretation was supported by Diarmaid MacCulloch in *The Later Reformation* (1990), who stated that 'already in the 1540s the old world was

Landmark Study   **The book that changed people's views**

Eamon Duffy, *The Voices of Morebath* (Yale, 2001)

Although this study covers the period 1520 to 1574, it is important in placing the impact of the English Reformation in context. The study of a small parish in Devon, through the eyes of its vicar, Sir Christopher Trychay, allows us to see how slowly the Reformation spread. There have been studies of counties, but never before have the records allowed us the opportunity to glimpse the progress at grass roots level. The picture is one of traditional pre-Reformation piety surviving long after Parliament had passed acts that abolished such practices. These findings support the arguments of the revisionist historians such as Haigh, who have argued that the Reformation was a slow process. It was only at the end of Trychay's life that he, and the village, accepted the changes. The book fully supports the arguments Duffy made in his other influential work, *The Stripping of the Altars* (Yale 1992). This was largely based on studies of East Anglia, and when the two books are considered together it becomes difficult to sustain the arguments of the traditional school that the Reformation was fast.

losing its enchantment'. It is therefore possible to suggest that, even if Protestantism had not taken hold at the grass roots, there were signs of a decline in affection for the old Church. Perhaps this is not surprising after the attacks of the previous decade.

How Protestant was England?

1. Read the following extract and answer the question.

   'The Act of Six Articles marked a decisive turning point for the progress of radical Protestantism under Henry. But the full scale of the reversal of evangelical fortunes was not at first evident. Cromwell remained all-powerful in the Council, and in the Spring of 1540 was created Earl of Essex. However, the fall of Cromwell undermined the confidence of the reformed attack on traditional religion.'

   (adapted from Eamon Duffy, *The Stripping of the Altars*, Yale, 1992)

   To what extent do you agree with Duffy's analysis of the nature and causes of change in the direction of religious policy in the last decade of Henry's rule?

2. Assess the reasons for Henry's divorce from Catherine of Aragon.

> **What were the aims of Henry's foreign policy?**

> **How successful was Wolsey in achieving Henry's aims?**

> **Was Henry's foreign policy after 1529 a costly mistake?**

Framework of events

1512	Henry declares war on France
1513	War against France, Battle of the Spurs
	Defeat of Scots at Battle of Flodden
1518	Treaty of London, peace between European powers
1520	Field of the Cloth of Gold
1521	Grand Enterprise against France brings little success
1525	Charles V captures Francis I, but also breaks agreement with Henry
1527	England join League of Cognac against the Empire
1532	Alliance with France
1538	Truce between France and Spain leads to fear of invasion
1542	Scotland is invaded. Battle of Solway Moss
1543	Henry allies with Charles and invades France

What were the aims of Henry's foreign policy?

In order to evaluate the success of Henry's foreign policy it is vital to be clear about his aims. There is little doubt that these changed during the course of his reign, although some general principles remained throughout the period. At the start of his reign, Henry was keen to assert himself on the European scene and be seen as a major force. The easiest way to do this was to abandon his father's peaceful policies and revive hostilities with France. Some historians have argued that there was a subtle change to the manner in which these aims would be achieved during the 1520s and that this change reflects the influence of his chief minister, Thomas Wolsey. Instead of war, Jack Scarisbrick, in *Henry VIII* (1968), argued that Wolsey pursued a policy of peace, as war was too expensive for England to sustain and went against his humanist principles. In this interpretation Wolsey strove to achieve glory for Henry through elaborate meetings and high-sounding peace treaties that were designed to keep England at the centre of European affairs.

There has also been great historical debate about who was actually in charge of policy and an understanding of this is important when trying to discern the aims, particularly if the King and his minister had different views. Contemporaries, such as the poet Thomas Skelton, believed that the real power was Wolsey's when he wrote that 'Hampton Court hath the pre-eminence' and this view was supported by the Venetian ambassador to England who wrote that 'the cardinal is the person who rules both the king and the entire kingdom'. However, Scarisbrick believed that, although it was often Wolsey alone who guided English affairs, the King could and did become furiously involved and that he had particular interests – largely foreign affairs. This view is supported by Paul Crowson, in *Tudor Foreign Policy* (1973), where he compared Henry to the creator and owner of a private business who has retired and left his affairs to a manager, but then rings him up three times a week to ensure that he is doing what the owner wants. Other historians have argued that the relationship was more like a partnership, but that the important decisions of war and peace rested with the King.

There is little doubt that the aims and direction of foreign policy changed in the late 1520s. This was because policy was dominated by Henry's desire for a divorce from Catherine of Aragon. Henry's main aim was to create a European situation in which the Pope could and would grant him a divorce. The result was a switch in the general direction of foreign policy away from friendship with Spain and the Holy Roman Empire, and towards France. The subsequent break with Rome also resulted in further changes. Henry's policy became less aggressive as he sought new allies against a possible joint Catholic crusade from the Habsburgs and Francis I. This defensive policy is best illustrated by the vast sums of money that were spent on fortifications along the south coast.

The final shift in policy came in the 1540s. The breakdown in Habsburg-French friendship meant that an invasion was unlikely and Henry was able to return to the aggressive policy that characterised his early years as he sought to assert himself on the continent and regain prestige. Unfortunately, the cost of these wars was vast, and would have serious consequences for later rulers.

The nature of Henry's foreign policy aims

Although there are general foreign policy aims which can be applied to any period –such as the protection of the realm from invasion – there are some that can be specifically applied to Henry's reign. These can be identified as follows:

- **Glory.** Henry wanted to establish England as a major power; although this proved difficult because she did not possess the resources or wealth of France or Spain. He also wanted to establish his own reputation as 'The most goodliest prince that ever reigned'.

- **Honour.** Henry was concerned about his personal honour and reputation. This was a medieval idea and, as with glory, Henry largely believed it this could be achieved through war. The idea of honour has been questioned by David Potter, in the article 'Foreign Policy' in *The Reign of Henry VIII: Politics, Policy and Piety* edited by MacCulloch. He argued that it was no more than rhetoric. However, it appears that it was a driving force in his relationship with Charles V and Francis I.

- **Conquest of France.** As a young boy Henry loved history and was inspired by stories of the mythical King Arthur and, particularly, of Henry V. His victory at Agincourt was an inspiration to Henry VIII.

- **The succession and securing the dynasty.** Henry was concerned throughout his reign to ensure that the Tudor dynasty was secure. This meant not only having a male heir, but also securing the marriage of his children to other European rulers, such as Mary to Charles V or Edward to Mary Queen of Scots.

- **Trade.** Although Henry VIII, unlike his father, is not usually seen as being interested in trade, this is not completely true as he was concerned to maintain good relations with the Netherlands throughout most of his reign because of the cloth trade with Antwerp.

- **Money.** Although most historians have not seen this as a priority, David Potter has argued that Henry was concerned to secure the French pension that his father had won and he has shown that this demand was present in all the wars Henry fought against France.

- **Imperial ambition.** Pollard argued that Henry had imperial ambitions and wanted to absorb Scotland into a 'Great Britain', but this view has largely been discredited by historians such as R. B. Wernham in *Before the Armada; the growth of English Foreign Policy 1485–1588* (1966), who argued that Henry was principally influenced by a dislike of the Scots and concern to protect the backdoor of England from invasion.

How successful was Wolsey in achieving Henry's aims?

The early years

Henry VIII's accession brought a change in the nature of English foreign policy. His priorities were very different from those of his father and contemporaries expected that the new King's aggression would soon find expression in a declaration of war as he sought to establish both himself and England on the international scene. A problem for Henry was that England lacked the resources for a long war against either of the European 'super-powers', France or Spain, but the opportunity came in 1511, when Henry joined the League of Cambrai against France and England became part of a war that was to last until 1514. However, Henry soon found out that European politics were not straightforward, as France was able to bribe England's intended allies and leave her isolated, resulting in failure. A similar failure was experienced in 1512, when Henry was tricked by his father-in-law, Ferdinand of Aragon, and his army was left to starve, whilst the Spanish achieved their goal in the Pyrenees. The English army returned home with nothing to show for an expensive adventure.

Wolsey's early years

Although Henry's early ventures had failed to achieve their goals, he was not prepared to abandon his ambitions. He realised that he could not rely on support from his allies and therefore the 1513 campaign was to be under his own personal command. **Thomas Wolsey** was given the task of organising the supplies and assembly

Thomas Wolsey (1472?–1529) The son of an Ipswich butcher, he was very able and went to Oxford, obtaining a degree at 15. His first appointment at	court was as almoner, but his organisational skills meant that he rose quickly. His breakthrough came when he successfully organised Henry's 1512 campaign to France. He was	appointed to a variety of bishoprics and became Lord Chancellor and Papal Legate, giving him a large amount of power, but he was unpopular with the nobility.

of the large force; he achieved this with great skill, showing Henry that he had outstanding administrative ability.

Such a large force could move only very slowly and the French were not prepared to meet them in a full-scale battle. As a result Henry was not able to achieve a decisive victory, but he did take the towns of Therouanne and Tournai. Therouanne was an unimportant town and was given to the Emperor Maximilian who proceeded to burn it, providing Henry with little gain or prestige. Tournai was different; it was an internationally known town and quickly fell to the English. More importantly, the skirmish with the French army, known as 'The Battle of the Spurs' could be portrayed as a great military victory (see page 42) as several French nobles were captured. However, most historians have been dismissive of the achievement. The campaign had used up nearly all the money that Henry VII had saved up and failed to do any significant damage to the French. Perhaps Catherine, in order to satisfy her husband's ego, offered him the only crumb of comfort when she commented that 'the victory hath been so great that I think none hath been seen before.'

Despite the limits of Henry's achievements, some historians have argued that the campaign did satisfy the King's aims of military leadership and valour. He had been able to lead an impressive force to France, secure a victory and have the Emperor serve under his flag. However, a comparison with events at home suggests that, on a wider scale, the French campaign was not significant. Whilst Henry was away fighting in France, the Scots had invaded England, only to be defeated at the Battle of Flodden. This was more significant as England had shown herself able to raise a second army. The results were even more dramatic as the Scottish King and many nobles were killed, with the result that Scotland was removed as a threat to the northern border for much of Henry's reign.

Henry wanted to continue his war in France in 1514, but the desertion of his allies and a lack of resources made it impossible. He had learnt that England was a second-rate power. It was Wolsey who was able to salvage some success for the King from the peace talks. Henry not only kept the territory he had captured, but also gained financially as the French King promised to pay the arrears from the French pension gained by Henry VII. The treaty also saw Henry marry his sister to the aged and toothless Louis XII of France. However, as Susan Doran argued in *England and Europe 1485–1603* (Longman 1986), Henry now had 'one sister as Queen of France and the other as Queen Regent of Scotland, his treasury was almost empty and his territorial gains were insignificant'.

0 — 800 km
0 — 500 miles

The 'Auld Alliance'

SCOTLAND

North Sea

DENMARK

BRANDENBERG

NETHERLANDS

SAXONY

ENGLAND

Calais • Antwerp

CLEVES

HOLY ROMAN EMPIRE

BOHEMIA

HUNGARY

AUSTRIA

FRANCE

Atlantic Ocean

BURGUNDY

MILAN

VENICE

OTTOMAN EMPIRE

PORTUGAL

SPAIN

ARAGON

PAPAL STATES

NAPLES

Mediterranean Sea

N

Western Europe c. 1530

Wolsey in charge 1514–1529

Although Henry still wanted to pursue an aggressive policy, Wolsey was aware that England could not afford such a war-like approach. Equally, he knew that if he wanted to stay in favour he had to provide Henry with success and glory. At first, Wolsey was unable to achieve this and by the end of 1517 little had been accomplished. The situation was made more desperate by the arrival of two new

Francis I (1494–1547)
King of France from
1515–1547. He was a
typical Renaissance Prince,
running a lavish court, but
also involved in a lifelong
rivalry with Charles V. As a
result he was at war with
Charles V for much of his
reign, particularly in Italy.
Henry usually fought against
Francis.

Treaty of London: A
treaty of universal peace
and friendship signed by
over 20 European rulers in
1518.

figures on the international scene, **Francis I** of France and Charles V of Habsburg (see page 20). These two young rulers also wanted to make a name for themselves, but unlike Henry, they had the resources available. Henry would be unable to challenge them in battle, therefore other ways had to be found.

Historians are divided about Wolsey's aims in this period. A. F. Pollard, in *Henry VIII* (1902), argued that Wolsey aimed to 'hitch England to the Holy See' in order to satisfy his own ambition to become Pope. This interpretation of England's policy in this period remained dominant until the 1960s, when an examination of the evidence by J. Scarisbrick made it hard to sustain. He argued that English policy was often in opposition to that of the papacy, that Wolsey trumped the Pope's call for a crusade in 1518 with his own **Treaty of London** and that he did not actively seek to become Pope until the King pushed him as a candidate. More recent work, particularly that by Dana Scott Campbell, in *English Foreign Policy 1509–1521* (1980), argued that Wolsey's aims were motivated by a desire for personal advancement. According to John Guy, in *Tudor England* (1988), the best way to achieve this was either to satisfy the King's claim to the French crown, or at least to enhance his prestige. As it was very difficult to achieve the former, Doran argued that Wolsey was very skilful as he 'placed Henry at the forefront of the international scene', not through warfare but diplomatic initiatives.

The Treaty of London

Although it is unclear who suggested that Henry tried to enhance his reputation through peace-making, it is probable that it was Wolsey. In order to achieve this he took over a papal initiative to raise troops against the Turks and turned it into an international treaty of peace and friendship. This culminated in the Treaty of London in October 1518. Henry was seen as the pivotal point in the new balance of

---

Landmark Study   The book that changed people's views

Jack Scarisbrick, *Henry VIII* (Methuen, 1968)

Scarisbrick's book was the first major biography since Pollard's study at the start of the twentieth century. His study saw the King return to centre stage, he dominated government and policy making, both at home and overseas. Although there were times, Scarisbrick argues, when ministers did make decisions there were times when Henry 'could break into his minister's conduct of affairs with decisive results'. According to Scarisbrick's argument Henry's involvement explains many of the uncertainties of the reign, particularly the process of the Reformation, since Henry himself was full of uncertainties. However, Scarisbrick's main concern was to show that ministers were the executants of the King's plans. According to this interpretation, if there was ever a blue-print for action it was provided by the King.

power, as Wolsey arranged for each of the signatories to sign the treaty separately with England, rather than all signing together. Contemporaries commented that it was a diplomatic triumph and brought considerable glory on Henry as leading European states agreed to perpetual peace. P. Crowson, in *Tudor Foreign Policy* (1973), commented that 'Wolsey offered [Henry] the enormous prestige of leading Europe towards humanistic peace', whilst Scarisbrick argued that it was 'to be the master document, committing Europe to a new principle in her diplomatic life, namely that of collective security'. Doran called it a 'glittering success', but perhaps glitter is all it was, because as T. A. Morris argued in *Europe and England in the Sixteenth Century* (1998), the Treaty was 'wholly at the mercy of shifts in great power politics over which England exercised no control'. Other historians have argued that Wolsey also sacrificed earlier gains by agreeing to the return of Tournai to the French as part of the deal for them signing the agreement.

The Field of the Cloth of Gold

The success of the Treaty of London was short-lived however, as once Charles Habsburg had been elected Holy Roman Emperor the balance of European power shifted dramatically. Wolsey worked hard to maintain England's high profile in international affairs. Charles V visited England in May 1520 and Henry and Francis met just outside Calais, at the Field of the Cloth of Gold, in June. Once again the splendour of the occasion did much to boost England and Henry's prestige. The meeting was spectacular; the palace that was constructed for Henry and his leading courtiers was described as one of the wonders of the age. Over eleven days sporting competitions took place between the two sets of nobles and even the Kings. Although both Kings did well in the jousting, Henry was beaten by Francis in a wrestling match, much to his annoyance.

Although there was supposed to be more to the meeting than a mere sporting match, nothing of significance was achieved and no agreements were reached. Henry may have been pleased with the honour that the meeting brought him, but if the aim was to reinforce the peace agreed at London, it was a failure because within two years England and France were at war with each other again.

Soon after the meeting Henry met Charles again and an agreement was signed that neither side would make a separate peace with France. Although it committed England to very little, it suggested that the agreement reached at London two years earlier had broken down and that its success had been short-lived. This was made clear

The Field of the Cloth of Gold, showing the splendour and image of power and wealth that the meeting created.

in 1521 when Francis and Charles were at war again. Therefore, if Wolsey had hoped that England would act as a counter weight between France and the Emperor, he had failed. England was not strong enough to be considered of importance and, as Starkey has argued, was trying to box above her weight.

War with France

In 1521 Wolsey reached an agreement with the Emperor that England would invade France unless France made peace with the Holy Roman Empire. Some historians have argued that Wolsey genuinely believed the threat of English support would be enough to force France into making peace, but this appears unlikely and others have suggested that he thought the war would be over before England had to act. In the event, England was forced to act and an army was sent to France in 1523. The campaign failed. It cost £400,000 with nothing to be seen for it, making it very unpopular at home. Henry had also lost the prestige that his earlier role as peace-maker had brought. At the same time, he had been abandoned by his allies. Wolsey was forced to look for peace.

The Battle of Pavia

However, just as quickly the international situation changed again. Charles V not only conquered Milan, but also captured Francis at the Battle of Pavia in 1525. Henry quickly saw this as the ideal opportunity to gain the French throne. He ordered Wolsey to raise the necessary finances and to organise a large force ready for an invasion in conjunction with Charles. However, the heavy taxation from the previous campaigns meant that Wolsey was unable to raise the taxes and he had to abandon the plan (see Chapter 3, page 49). He had failed his master, there would be no invasion or French crown to satisfy Henry's dreams.

The wars of the 1520s had brought no recognisable gains. Henry had been deserted by the Emperor in 1522 and 1523 and financial shortages had prevented him from taking advantage of the favourable international situation in 1525. Once again it appeared as if England was a minor power on the European stage. Although Wolsey had managed some short-term shows of prestige for the King, little that was tangible had been achieved. In many ways it is unfair to criticise Wolsey for failing the King; he had been asked to do the impossible as England simply lacked the resources to be a major power. At times he had been able to enhance Henry's status, but it was through diplomatic events, rather than war. When Wolsey was able to involve England in European conflict and satisfy the King's desire for military glory, it was because Charles V saw how Henry could be used to divert French resources away from Italy. England was only a pawn in a bigger game. Wolsey had tried his best to enhance England's status, but at best this was achieved only in the short term.

The war also resulted in a change in direction in English foreign policy. England abandoned Charles and in August 1525 made an alliance with France. This was reinforced in 1526 and again in 1527. England would not go to war with France again until 1543. However, a more pressing concern was to dominate Wolsey's last years.

The divorce

Henry' desire for a divorce from Catherine of Aragon, discussed in Chapter 1, dominated foreign policy from 1527 to Wolsey's fall and beyond. The capture of the Pope by Habsburg troops made him a virtual prisoner and as a result Wolsey had to find a way of restoring the Pope's independence. In order to achieve this England agreed to help fund a French attack in Italy. Wolsey also **suspended trade with the Netherlands** in an attempt to force Charles to allow the Pope to agree to the divorce. However, the policy was a failure both at home and overseas. At home there were large-scale protests from the cloth industry and this forced Wolsey to abandon the policy. Meanwhile in Italy, Francis was pushed back and was forced to make peace with Charles. Henry was now isolated and the last chance of gaining the support of the Pope for a divorce had gone. The international situation meant that Wolsey faced an impossible task. However, although it is unfair to blame Wolsey for the failure of the policy, his inability to achieve the divorce led to his fall in October 1529.

Trade with the Netherlands: The cloth trade with the Netherlands, particularly Antwerp, was vital to England. Any interruptions resulted in large-scale unemployment in England.

Was Henry's foreign policy after 1529 a costly mistake?

Much of the last years of Henry's reign were spent at war and as the cost was over £2 million, or ten year's worth of regular income, it is easy to see why historians have considered this period a costly mistake. Henry had spent nearly all the money acquired from the Dissolution of the Monasteries, he had debased the coinage, encouraging inflation, and in return the only gain was Boulogne. However, the role of a monarch, particularly Henry, was to wage war and he had been able to achieve his wish. Is it therefore fair to judge his policy against modern standards or should it be judged against his aims?

The 1530s and the Reformation

For much of the 1530s Henry was more concerned with domestic issues (see Chapter 3). His foreign policy was largely defensive and a reaction to the fear of invasion from Charles V or even a Catholic crusade. However, he was fortunate that Charles was occupied by his struggle against the Turks in the east and that Francis was more concerned to try and regain lands lost in Italy.

Throughout most of the 1530s Henry's Principal Minister Cromwell, who had survived Wolsey's demise, ensured that Henry followed a less warlike policy, yet even this brought costs. The ten-year truce between Charles and Francis, signed in 1538, made the possibility of an invasion more likely. As a result Henry had little choice but to use some of the money gained from the Dissolution of the Monasteries to develop fortifications along the south coast. It also forced him to look for other European allies and it resulted in talks with the German Protestant princes who made up the Schmalkaldic League. The result was Henry's fourth marriage, to the Protestant Anne of Cleves. Although this was not financially costly, Henry soon saw it as a mistake. As soon as he met Anne he declared, 'If I had known as much before as I know now, she should never have come into this realm'. Doran has even suggested that if Charles had not been meeting Francis on the same day as the wedding, it is unlikely that it would have taken place. However, no sooner had the marriage taken place than the need for it was removed as the alliance between France and the Emperor collapsed.

With the benefit of hindsight it is easy to argue that the chances of an invasion were never great, but Henry felt vulnerable and was prepared to marry Anne to protect the nation's security.

War with Scotland

Much of the last years of Henry's reign were spent at war with either France or Scotland. It appears that the trigger to war in 1542 was James V's failure to attend an arranged meeting with Henry at York in 1541. Henry took this failure personally and considered that he had been insulted. However, according to Doran, he had other motives for launching an attack. Throughout the 1530s, when Henry needed support, James V had shown his loyalty was to France by twice marrying French princesses. He had also protected rebels who had fled following the defeat of the Pilgrimage of Grace. In 1542 Henry therefore ordered a raid on Scotland, which resulted in a resounding victory at Solway Moss. Ten days later James V died, supposedly from shame at the scale of the defeat. This left a one-week old girl, Mary, as

The campaign of 1513: Henry's meeting with Maximilian, the 'Battle of the Spurs' and the siege of Tournai.

Queen. At first it appeared as if Henry would triumph and be able to solve the Scottish problem once and for all.

Henry chose to solve the problem not by invading but through peaceful means, the marriage of Mary to his son Edward. According to Wernham, Henry chose not to invade because he feared that the French would use the opportunity to attack, but Doran disagrees and argues that Francis did not want war with England because he was about to attack Charles. According to this interpretation Henry now had the ideal chance to conquer Scotland.

Instead, in order to persuade the Scots to accept the marriage plan, Henry gave his Scottish prisoners large presents and released them with the instruction to advance his cause at home. Initially the marriage was agreed by The Treaties of Greenwich in 1543, but the Scots declined to hand over Mary and then, at the end of the year, the Scottish Parliament rejected the Treaties. Henry had lost his opportunity and a great deal of money in bribes. He now decided to resort to force and sent the Earl of Hertford on a series of raids, known as the 'rough-wooing', in which Edinburgh and other towns were set alight.

It is hardly surprising that this failed to win over Scottish minds but served only to reinforce their hatred of the English. Mary, instead of marrying Edward was to be married to the Dauphin, the eldest son of Francis I of France. This would only reinforce the Auld Alliance and was later to cause Elizabeth I problems. Despite the defeat of the Scots at Solway, Henry had also failed to destroy them as a potential military threat, as they were still able to launch raids across the border when England was vulnerable.

It is difficult to construct a defence of Henry's actions. Perhaps the best that can be argued is that Scotland did not launch an attack in 1544 or 1545 when England was at war with France. However, it is probably unfair to criticise Henry for not invading after the death of James and seizing Mary. It is unlikely that the Scots would ever have allowed the English to capture Mary. But, whatever conclusion is reached, it is difficult to see the actions as anything but failure. On the one hand it can be argued that Henry lost a winning position after 1542; on the other hand it was a failure because his aims were unrealistic.

War with France

Although many historians have argued that the wars with France brought as little gain as the wars with Scotland, it is possible to argue that compared to the other European rulers of the period, who had far larger resources available, Henry did relatively well. The war with France did result in the gain of Boulogne in 1544 and, although the financial cost was great, Henry was the only ruler to achieve a major military victory in this period. He must also have been pleased that after earlier betrayals by his supposed allies he had been able to achieve this alone and show that England was a military force. Not only was he able to hold on to this gain in the Peace of Ardres in 1546, but France also agreed to pay all outstanding pensions. Therefore, judging Henry against his own aims of glory and honour, it can be argued that he had achieved his goals.

However, the cost of this campaign cannot be ignored. The wars had cost over £2 million and, according to Diarmaid MacCulloch in *The Reign of Henry VIII: Politics, Policy and Piety*, Henry had 'engineered a mid-Tudor crisis even if fate had not stepped in with epidemics and wretched harvests in the Edwardian and Marian years'. The wars had used up the money gained from the Dissolution, and had led to the debasement of the coinage (and all the problems that would cause), large-scale borrowing on the Antwerp money market, heavy taxation and forced loans

At the same time, England was without allies as the Habsburgs had made peace with France, leaving Francis free to launch an English invasion. This situation was made worse by the result of his Scottish policy, which had left the Scots eager for revenge. As a result the French fleet was able to enter the Solent, but fortunately got no further than a small raiding party landing on the Isle of Wight. Although Henry was able to keep Boulogne, the cost of the wars hardly justified the gain, even in prestige.

An assessment

England was not a powerful country in this period and it was very hard for Henry to achieve his aims. It is therefore important to be clear which criteria we are using in assessing the success of his foreign policy. Henry would have maintained that he had fulfilled a monarch's obligation to wage war and bring glory on the nation. It is true that there were occasions when national prestige was gained, with the Treaty of London and the Field of the Cloth of Gold, but these were usually short-lived. There were also some notable victories on the battlefield at Flodden and Solway Moss, and in the capture of Boulogne and Tournai, but the cost was immense with over £3.5 million being spent on war during the course of his reign. His policy towards Scotland created even deeper hostility and failed to achieve its aims, whilst his gains in France were short-term and very costly. However, although there were short-term threats to national security, as in 1545, Henry was able to successfully protect the country's independence, even after the Break with Rome.

How successful was Henry's foreign policy?

1. Read the following extract and answer the question.

   'The king took a more consistent and informed interest in foreign policy than in other areas of government, and this both eased and complicated Wolsey's task. King and cardinal could work as a very effective double act. But at all times the most significant decisions, above all those of war and peace, rested with the king, and Wolsey never questioned the fact; indeed he found it politic to refer to all the best ideas on policy, whatever their origin, as Henry's own.'

   (Adapted from S.J. Gunn and P. G. Lindley, *Cardinal Wolsey: Church, State and Art*, Cambridge University Press, 1991)

   How accurate is this assessment of the role of Wolsey and Henry in matters of foreign policy?

2. Assess the view that Henry's foreign policy was more successful under Wolsey than after Wolsey's fall.

Was Henry a Tyrant?

Did Henry
introduce a new
style of kingship?

How well was
Henry served by his
ministers?

How far was Henry
threatened by
rebellion and
unrest?

Was Henry
manipulated by
faction in the
1540s?

Framework of events

1510	Wolsey appointed a royal councillor
1515	Wolsey appointed Lord Chancellor
1523	Wolsey fails to persuade Parliament to grant money for war against France
1525	Amicable Grant rebellion
1527–9	Wolsey attempts to gain Henry a divorce
1530	Death of Wolsey on his way to be tried for treason
	Thomas Cromwell joins the Council
1534	Cromwell is made Vice-Regent in ecclesiastical affairs and Lord Privy Seal
1535	Pilgrimage of Grace
1540	Execution of Thomas Cromwell. Henry marries Catherine Howard.
1542	Execution of Catherine Howard for adultery
1543	Henry marries Catherine Parr
1546	Triumph of reform faction

HISTORIANS have disagreed strongly over what type of king Henry was. The image from the Holbein paintings (see page 7) shows a king who personifies power, strength and authority; whereas the Matsys portrait of 1544 (shown opposite), has been used to argue that he was mean, mad and power crazed.

Traditional accounts of Henry's reign have often portrayed him as a tyrant. These interpretations have particularly used the last years of his reign to show that he was a bully who abused his power, punishing those who disagreed with him and even allowing his queen, Catherine Parr, to be arrested on charges of heresy. During

Portrait of Henry by Cornelius Matsys, painted in 1544. It shows the bloated Henry of latter years compared with the earlier Holbein works.

the 1530s, when the Reformation was being introduced, some have argued that he operated a 'reign of terror' and that by extending the Treason Act of 1534 to include words he had the power to remove any potential opposition, or at least terrify opponents into silence. These accounts have also argued that Henry seemed to gain pleasure from making his victims squirm or by making them plead for mercy. Perhaps the biggest indictment of Henry was his treatment of former ministers and queens, who were removed when they had served their purpose, often on trumped-up charges.

More recent work has suggested that in many instances Henry was a much weaker King than traditional accounts have argued. Although most historians would still agree that his last years brought little benefit to the country, there is much debate about whether Henry was in control of events, and some interpretations have portrayed him as little more than a bystander who was manipulated by court factions. Although Henry could be severe to enemies and potential enemies, it must be remembered that, without a police force to uphold law and order, there were times when an example had to be made. The numbers killed as a result of his Reformation were no greater than those under Mary and were certainly less than those on the continent. The challenges of the Amicable Grant unrest and the

Pilgrimage of Grace also suggest that he was not the all-powerful King of popular legend, but a ruler who, like other Tudors, needed the support of the political nation if his policies were to be enforced. Henry may have raised the status of the monarchy and his own image, but in practice his power was limited. Historians still remain divided over his achievements and it is unlikely that a consensus will be reached as they balance his treatment of those around him against the changes made in government and to the Church.

Did Henry introduce a new style of kingship?

Renaissance: A term used to describe European history from the fourteenth to the seventeenth centuries. It involved the re-discovery of classical literature and a study of man.

Some historians have seen in Henry the emergence of a new style of kingship, closely associated with the **Renaissance** and the idea of the 'universal man'. This interpretation is based on his love of music, languages and sport. However, other accounts have argued that his kingship was closer to that of the medieval monarch who was concerned with warfare, and the chivalric values of courage and honour. It appeared as if he modelled his court on Burgundy, where the idea of the perfect knight was fashionable. Certainly, however, there was a change in style from the rule of his father.

Bonds and recognisances: Henry VII made many nobles agree to these in order to ensure their loyalty. A bond bound one person to another; if they broke the bond they had to pay a sum of money. A recognisance was a formal acknowledgement of a debt and could be enforced through a heavy fine.

Henry VII's reign had ended with the monarchy unpopular. There is little doubt that the nobility and gentry, faced with the financial pressures of **bonds and recognisances,** were close to revolt. Henry VIII was undoubtedly keen to distance himself from the old regime and had Richard Empson and Robert Dudley, two of the most hated advisors and enforcers, arrested and executed in what have been described as 'show trials'. It can therefore be argued that Henry was already showing a ruthless side, or that he realised the value of winning popularity and would take whatever steps were needed to gain it. John Guy argued that the executions 'were a calculated ploy to enable the new regime to profit from the stability won by Henry VII'. All of these characteristics would surface again later in the reign, but it did not augur well for his advisors! David Starkey argued, in his television programme *Henry VIII*, that he had taken the advice of the book his tutor, John Skelton, had written for him, 'Speculum Principis' or 'The Mirror for a Prince'. In this book he told Henry that he could not rest easy with his status and that he should trust no-one. Skelton also reminded Henry of the fate of many of his predecessors and that the only way to avoid it was to do the job himself, rather than trust councillors. It appeared as if the reign had started from this premise.

This attitude appeared to be reinforced in 1513, when Edmund de la Pole, nephew of Edward IV, was executed. His brother, Richard, had taken up arms in support of the French against England and Henry feared that Edmund might join him or use the opportunity to relaunch the Yorkist claim to the throne. Henry would not tolerate real or potential opposition and this was also shown in his decision to maintain many of the unpopular bonds of Henry VII's reign.

It would appear that Henry's attitude to kingship was a combination of both medieval and Renaissance ideals, a man of his time. There is little doubt that he wanted to be a warrior King, as argued in Chapter 2, but he also wanted to be an Imperial King, with ideas that dated back to the Roman Empire, and that would raise his status and image. Even if there were undoubtedly times when he was a weak King, it is possible to argue that these were the very times he needed to show tyrannical power to try and convince others of his authority and importance.

How far was Henry threatened by rebellion and unrest?

If traditional accounts of an all-powerful King are correct, it is unlikely that Henry would have been seriously challenged by rebellion or unrest. However, it can be argued that the two major rebellions Henry faced (see below) were the most challenging of any Tudor monarch, forcing him to abandon policies that were dear to his heart. Both rebellions saw the involvement of large numbers of the population, over a geographically wide area, and, probably most worryingly for Henry, they both gained support from a variety of social classes. Henry was forced to issue pardons to both sets of rebels and, at the same time, to publicly humiliate his leading ministers of the time.

The Amicable Grant

Charles V's victory at Pavia (see page 39) gave Henry the chance to further his claim to the French throne. However, in order to achieve this he needed vast sums of money which could only be obtained through Parliament. Wolsey's plan to achieve this was the so-called Amicable Grant. The auspices were not good, as the loan of 1522–3 had not been repaid and the subsidy of 1523 was still being collected. It is therefore not surprising that there was severe resistance to the Grant and collectors met with considerable opposition. Nor did it help the collectors that Henry's foreign policy had brought little tangible gain. Wolsey was forced to back down and instead ask for voluntary contributions. However, this did not prevent the outbreak of full-scale resistance in East Anglia and 10 000 men were assembled at Lavenham. They realised that the government had already been forced to back down and that if they continued to resist they might gain further concessions. The rebels were only dispersed by the actions of the local nobility.

At the same time, opposition in London also weakened the King's position. Henry was forced to abandon his policy. Although it was Wolsey who was blamed for the tax and had to make an apology to the rebels, it was Henry whose prestige had suffered. The levying of the tax had made both Wolsey and the King unpopular with the political and propertied classes of England. This retreat showed that they could not be ignored and that, although earlier attempts to raise money for war had been successful, there were limits to how far the political nation could be pushed. Tired of the disruption that war brought to economic life, the **commons** of East Anglia had reminded the King that he needed their co-operation and that government was still based on a partnership between government and governed. Innovation could go only so far. This shows that when the Crown was robbed of its traditional supporters it was vulnerable, because it was usually this group who defended the monarchy against disorder.

Commons: The ordinary people, not nobles

The Pilgrimage of Grace

During the autumn and winter of 1536–7 Henry was faced with the largest rebellion of the Tudor period when 40,000 rebels assembled, known as the **Pilgrimage of Grace**. Although traditional accounts portray the rebellion as a failure and use the massacre at Carlisle and subsequent retributions in 1537 to support their interpretation, more recent work by Michael Bush in 'The Pilgrimage of Grace' (Manchester University Press, 1996), has shown that the rebellion cannot be dismissed as a failure. His interpretation of events supports the view that in the latter months of 1536 Henry was in a very weak position and that it was only the foolish **Bigod Rising** of early 1537 that allowed him to regain the initiative.

At first sight it does appear that the traditional interpretation of the Pilgrimage as just another failed Tudor rebellion is correct and that the scale of retribution that followed illustrates the power of the Tudor monarchy to inspire fear. The rebels failed to prevent the closure of the remaining monasteries, as religious houses had gone by 1540. Also, the main target of their complaints, Thomas Cromwell, was still in power and political power was still centralised in London, despite the call for a northern parliament.

Pilgrimage of Grace: The rebellion was thought by many historians to have been caused by Henry closing the monasteries. More recent studies point to a complex combination of factors including social and economic as well as religious issues.

Bigod Rising: Sir Francis Bigod did not trust Henry's promises made to disperse the Pilgrimage and led a new rising in the north of England in early 1537. He was captured in Cumberland and the rebels were massacred at Carlisle.

However, the work of Bush has argued that the rebellion should be seen as far more successful. There is no doubt that the rebel army of 40 000 could have defeated the royal army of 8 000 that Henry could muster. It was only because this was not the aim of the rebel leadership that Henry survived. It was the pilgrims who chose to have a negotiated settlement in both October and December 1536. The King was forced into talks with the rebel leadership and the settlement that was reached was a massive climbdown for the government. They had been forced into this because they did not have the force to disperse the rebels. As a result all the rebels, even the leaders, received a free pardon. At the same time, specific grievances were settled and a study of the direction of religious reform after the rising suggests that the rebellion stopped, or at least slowed down, the rate of religious change. The rebels also stopped the collection of the subsidy and achieved their **agrarian aims** with entry fines set according to their wishes. As Bush concludes, 'in these respects, then, the formation of the pilgrim armies in October 1536 has to be appreciated not only as a spectacular achievement in itself but also a major influence upon religious, political, fiscal and agrarian changes of the time'.

Agrarian aims: Some of the rebels had particular agricultural concerns, including enclosure and the level of entry fines — that is, the sum they had to pay when taking up a new lease on land, usually following the death of the previous tenant.

Without the Bigod Rising of 1537 one is left wondering what would have happened, since it was that rising which gave Henry the excuse he needed to break his promises of the previous autumn and exact revenge. However, the rebellion showed that when a wide range of social groups rose, particularly if they included the ruling class, the monarchy was in serious trouble. Once again it showed that Henry needed the support of the local nobility if he was to enforce his policies. Equally, it is possible to argue that the death toll of 178 which followed the rebel defeat at Carlisle, and the loss by the Earl of Northumberland of his lands, show the ruthlessness of the King. Yet this is not the whole story, as Henry realised that he did not have full control in the north and as a result he set about reorganising the Council of the North so that royal authority could be enforced.

How well was Henry served by his ministers?

The popular image of Henry is of a man who enjoyed the good things in life – hunting, jousting and entertainment – but considered that the government of the country was tedious and a distraction from what he would rather be doing. He was fortunate that from 1514 to 1540 he was served by two ministers, Thomas Wolsey and Thomas Cromwell, who were prepared to run the country for him.

Thomas Wolsey

Wolsey had risen to prominence through his organisation of Henry's early campaigns in France, where he had shown himself to be an able administrator and planner. An assessment of his foreign policy achievements is considered in Chapter 2, but there are other areas where Wolsey also played a key role and which need to be considered if an overall judgement of him is to be made. Whilst in power he was a controversial figure and he continues to be the subject of much debate among historians. Most of his contemporaries were hostile towards him; Edward Hall criticised him because he personified all the ills of the old Catholic church and when he had the chance to reform it, he failed. This critical view was reinforced by Elton, who argued that he was 'amateurish and uncreative in the government of the realm and only moderately successful in ruling its church'. John Guy, writing in 1988, was more balanced, arguing that Wolsey was the consummate politician, but that 'his vision and originality in Star Chamber were limited by his personality; his management of parliament in 1523 was ham-handed; his success in realising the monetary potential was seriously reduced by the debacle of the Amicable Grant'.

There is little doubt that Henry thought a great deal of Wolsey, which was why he was able to survive for so long. As John Guy argued, 'Henry treated him more as a partner than a servant. Wolsey enjoyed uniquely privileged access to the king'. He did bring about some achievements in the fields of law, finance and the economy, but how far-reaching these were, is a matter for debate. He helped to modernise the legal system; the reform of **Star Chamber** was a success if judged by the increased workload, and it provided an efficient system that was both fair and cheap. He encouraged ordinary people to bring cases against the nobility, and although it may have made him unpopular with the latter, it meant that justice was open to all.

Star Chamber: A legal court, so called because the ceiling had stars painted on it.

Wolsey also played an important role in the area of tax reform. He created a new tax, the subsidy, which was flexible in its demands and based on accurate valuations of the payer's wealth. It was so successful that it brought in £300 000 on the four occasions it was levied between 1513–15 and 1523, allowing Henry to pursue his aggressive foreign policy. However, his demands for money in 1525 led to the Amicable Grant rebellion and caused Henry to start to lose confidence in his minister. Wolsey's economic policy was less successful and was unpopular with the nobility and landed classes. This was because of his attack on **enclosure**. He established a

Enclosure: By this process, large fields had hedges put round them, which made it possible to use more efficient farming techniques. However, some of the gentry and nobles enclosed common land so the peasants lost out.

commission to examine the extent of the problem and how people had been affected, and when it reported back he launched cases against over 260 landlords. However, he was forced to abandon this in return for a large subsidy from Parliament in 1523.

There is little doubt that Wolsey's failure to obtain Henry a divorce was the ultimate cause of his downfall. Although the failure was largely due to events beyond his control, this did not save him because Henry, encouraged by the Boleyn faction, believed that Wolsey was deliberately delaying the case. However, Henry's actions in the last months of Wolsey's life, when he was given tokens of the King's estimation, suggest that he was still considering keeping him. This interpretation would also suggest that it was the Boleyn faction who played a large role in the downfall of the cardinal and Henry soon regretted getting rid of the minister who was best able to carry out his wishes.

Thomas Cromwell

Thomas Cromwell began his rise to power working for Wolsey and became his secretary. However, it was his work in persuading Henry to declare himself Head of the Church which saw his rapid promotion to the Privy Council in 1531. He would effectively be the King's chief minister until his fall in 1540. Historians agree that Cromwell did not have the same degree of freedom that Wolsey had enjoyed, but it is possible to argue that he was instrumental in bringing about changes which had a far greater effect than those of Wolsey. Until the 1950s Cromwell was seen as an unpleasant figure, described by Keith Randell in *Henry VIII and the Government of England* (Hodder 1991) as a hatchet man, who received his just deserts in 1540 when he was abandoned and judicially murdered by his master. These accounts argued that to control opposition to the religious changes of the 1530s he created a ruthless system of repression based on spies, and that it resulted in thousands of innocent victims being put to death.

However, the work of Geoffrey Elton, particularly in *Tudor Revolution in Government* (see Landmark Study), has argued that the changes of the 1530s were masterminded by Cromwell as he modernised English government and left a legacy that went far beyond the achievements of Wolsey. In the short term he had helped Henry to: obtain a divorce; increase his power over the Church; and obtain vast sums of wealth. However, this interpretation also stresses the long-term changes he brought about in the whole system of government and how the country was administered, as well as how

G. R. Elton, *Tudor Revolution in Government* (Cambridge, 1953)

Perhaps no other book has done as much to shape our understanding of Tudor government, particularly the 1530s, and to place Thomas Cromwell at the centre of a change that saw England move from being a medieval monarchy to a modern system of government that is recognisable today. Elton argued that before this time the government of England was personal, based on the monarch and a few servants and with no bureaucracy. However, the changes brought about by Cromwell created a more centralised administration, reforming the financial running of the country and putting the Council at the centre of affairs. Although much of Elton's argument has been destroyed by critics such as Penry Williams and G. Harriss, in an article entitled 'A Revolution in Tudor History?', it still provides a framework against which to judge the achievements of Cromwell, and as J. Scarisbrick comments, 'never before had England felt the power of the state so widely and deeply as in the 1530s and 1540s', suggesting that the changes were far reaching, even if they do not amount to a revolution.

the country worshipped and paid its taxes. Cromwell also revolutionised the role of Parliament; this was central to the changes of the 1530s as statute law became supreme and Parliament took on new responsibilities in framing ecclesiastical changes. At the same time Wales was more closely linked to English ways through the Act of Union of 1536 and the independence of the north was reduced, making England a more unified nation. The religious changes also allowed Cromwell to make the Crown financially independent of Parliament. New financial courts were established to administer monastic incomes, and this gave Henry the opportunity to follow his own foreign policy interests in the 1540s.

Despite the fact that these achievements were pushed through by one man and in a short space of time, 1532–40, most historians have dismissed Elton's claims. They have argued that neither the nature, nor the extent of the changes, deserved to be called revolutionary. They have also argued that too much of the credit was given to Cromwell. However, much of the debate depends upon the use of the term 'revolution'. Some historians have argued that Cromwell was simply returning to old practices, whilst David Loades, in *Politics and the Nation* (Batsford, 1964), argued that Cromwell simply made existing systems work and did not create new structures. However, a careful reading of many of Cromwell's critics shows that it is impossible to ignore his achievements. Loades comments on his achievements in finance, the Privy Council and Council of Wales and the north. John Guy, having argued that more credit should be given to Wolsey for his achievements in reforming the Privy Council, produces a list of the changes Cromwell brought about in government and administration, referring to him as 'an administrator of genius'.

Henry meeting with
Parliament in 1523. He
flattered Parliament by
claiming that his power
was never so great as
when he met with them.

Although historians might disagree about whether these changes deserve to be called revolutionary, they are agreed about his ability, his skill and the lasting legacy of his work. It is possible to suggest that it was his work in reforming government that allowed the Tudor state to survive the challenges of a minor ruler and a female ruler. In creating him Earl of Essex, Henry had clearly shown his regard for him, as it was very unusual to elevate to the senior peerage a man who had no noble connections. Cromwell's fall was the result of Henry's entanglement with Catherine Howard (see page 56). It was soon followed by realisation and anger that he had been tricked by Cromwell's enemies and Henry was full of remorse for the execution of a man who had served him so well.

Was Henry manipulated by faction in the 1540s?

Until quite recently historical research had largely ignored the 1540s, as the only events deemed worthy of consideration were those associated with foreign policy. For many historians it was obvious that, from the fall of Thomas Cromwell in 1540 until Henry's death in 1547, the country slid downhill though a series of crises which were caused by a King who had become increasingly tyrannical and out-of-touch with reality. Scarisbrick described it as the 'years of ruthless jockeying by ruthless men'. Faction dominated and, according to Ives, this weakened the King's control and left him a victim of the struggles. It also meant that decisions were often slow, which caused further chaos, or were made so rapidly that they were based on unrealistic assumptions.

Although no historian has tried to argue that the last years of Henry's reign were a time of success or benefit for the country, there has been some modification of the traditional picture. However, according to A. G. R. Smith, the factional struggles of the 1540s can be used to show that the King was fully aware of his courtiers' attempts to manipulate him. According to this interpretation Henry enjoyed watching the struggle for his attention, but it is also possible to argue that Henry managed successfully to follow a policy of divide and rule, where no one group was allowed to dominate policy making, and that discussion was actually encouraged. As a result, Henry can be judged less harshly and seen as a monarch who was in control of events until the last year, when illness did see others acting on his behalf.

Henry's marriage to Catherine Howard

Most historians have used Henry's marriage to Catherine Howard to show that he had lost touch with reality and was being manipulated by court faction. There is little doubt that Henry was 'set up' by the Norfolk faction as they sought to remove Cromwell and the other lowly-born councillors who surrounded the King and replace them with his proper advisors, the nobility. When Henry was introduced to Catherine, at the home of Stephen Gardiner, he quickly fell in love with her and was soon showering her with gifts and promoting her relatives. The plan appeared to have worked.

However, Catherine soon became bored with Henry and lacked the political skill to pretend that she loved him. Although Henry probably did not notice his wife's behaviour, opponents of the Howards and the Catholic faction did. They were quick to seize the initiative and Cranmer handed Henry information about his wife's indiscretions. The opposition were so concerned about Henry's reaction and behaviour that they chose Cranmer, the King's most trusted servant, to deliver the news, but even then it was done in a sealed envelope, during a church service and with the message not to read the contents until later.

The fall of Catherine Howard

Henry's initial reaction was disbelief but confessions from some of those involved with his wife forced him to admit reality. He had been gullible in failing to see through the Howard plan, but he also learnt from his mistakes. The King did not wreak full vengeance from the Howards; the Queen, the female head of the household and two men implicated were executed, but Norfolk and his associates escaped punishment. Norfolk had been a loyal servant of the King throughout the period, had followed the King's wishes and was now in his seventies. Henry's decision to allow him to remove himself from court does not give the impression of a King who was callous and always desirous of revenge. The King also showed that he was a realist in the choice of his final wife, Catherine Parr, who provided support for Henry and his children in his final years, doing much to reunite the family.

Charges against Thomas Cranmer and Catherine Parr

Thomas Cranmer had been a loyal servant to Henry in the 1530s, declaring his marriage to Catherine of Aragon null and void and secretly marrying him to Anne Boleyn. However, in 1543 he became the next victim of the factional struggle that dominated the 1540s. The conservative faction attacked him as a heretic and Henry had him arrested and sent to the Tower. It appeared as if he was about to follow the same path as Cromwell.

However, as in the Norfolk case, Henry stood by a trusted servant. According to Scarisbrick, Henry warned Cranmer of the plot, gave him a ring as a sign of trust and told him to produce it and demand to be heard by the King when arrested. The King then ordered Cranmer to investigate the charges himself. This meant that the accusers faced the prospect of being judged by the very person they wanted to convict. It is hardly surprising that the case was dropped. There is little doubt that Henry was in full control, unwilling to be manipulated by faction, and prepared to stand by and protect a loyal servant. However, it can also be

Thomas Cranmer (1489–1556)
A priest who had been educated at Cambridge. He supported Henry's divorce from Anne Boleyn and was appointed Archbishop of Canterbury in 1533. He had Protestant sympathies.

argued that Henry was unable to disassociate himself from court intrigue – as Scarisbrick argued, he took pleasure in 'confounding others, neither now, nor later was he capable, apparently, of the simple and direct action of stamping out conspiracy when he first heard of it'. Cranmer survived, but he must have been terrified when he was arrested. It is therefore possible to argue that, although Henry was always in control, he also liked to see even loyal servants embarrassed and realise that they owed their survival to him.

This argument can also be supported by the events of 1546. The conservative faction wanted revenge following the fall, in 1542, of Henry's fifth wife. Henry's final wife was Catherine Parr. She was a sympathiser with the new religion and the conservative faction soon presented the King with evidence to show that Catherine's religious beliefs were closer to Luther's ideas than was allowed by the law. Catherine was arrested on charges of heresy and taken to the Tower for questioning. However, it appears that Henry ensured that Catherine was told about the charges because shortly afterwards she was able to see her husband and he accepted her promise to believe and follow what he wanted. However, the King did not tell Catherine's opponents and when they arrived to arrest the Queen they were greeted by a torrent of abuse from Henry for a treasonous act.

Although Henry had again shown that he was in control of events, he had subjected his wife to an unnecessary ordeal. These two events together give the impression that Henry did get some satisfaction from being devious. It could even be argued that he wanted to teach his wife a lesson – that even she was subordinate to him and that he was willing to bully her into acceptance of his views. However, it is also possible to argue that Henry was concerned to show both factions that he still decided policy.

The fall of Gardiner and Norfolk

The fall of these two men does show that, in many ways, the King was dominated by the reform faction in the last year of his reign. Gardiner had become involved in the plot to bring down Catherine Parr, but it was a trumped-up charge (that he refused to grant some of his lands to the King) that led to his fall. Having been involved in earlier struggles and only just escaped, it can be argued that his position was already in decline. However, the fact that he fell over such a minor issue does appear to support the argument that the reformers were achieving ascendancy at court and were able to remove all opposition from positions of influence.

Norfolk had been a loyal servant to Henry but in 1546 he was implicated in the treasonous plot of his son, the Earl of Surrey. Surrey had suggested that he had a good claim to the throne of England and had also put part of the royal coat-of-arms of his ancestor, Edward I, on his family emblem without permission. In the circumstances it is understandable that there was concern he was serious in his designs on the crown. As Henry's successor was a young boy it is hardly surprising that Surrey was executed, although some historians have suggested that this is a further example of the King's paranoia. Norfolk was also arrested and would have been executed had not Henry died before signing the warrant. Although luck was on Norfolk's side, his arrest, having survived earlier scares, does support the interpretation that Henry had lost control and that the reform faction had now gained the ascendancy.

This view is more convincing when an examination of two key appointments of the final years is made. Sir Anthony Denny was appointed to be in charge of the King's Privy Chamber and Sir William Paget was appointed as Henry's Private Secretary. These two men managed access to the King, Denny through control of access to the King's private rooms, and Paget through controlling the written information that reached the King. It can be argued that these two men therefore ensured the triumph of the reform faction and made certain that the plot to alter Henry's will and establish a Regency Council was successful. If this is true, faction did ultimately triumph in the 1540s, albeit only at the very end.

Although it appears that Henry's reign ended in failure, with a series of costly wars, a virtually bankrupt kingdom, religious division and a minor to inherit the crown, the King had done much to raise the majesty of monarchy. It was perhaps this legacy which ensured that Edward's succession was unchallenged and that law and order remained intact through both his reign and his half sister's. Indeed, it probably laid the foundation for the flowering of the Tudor monarchy under Elizabeth.

Was Henry a tyrant?

1. Read the following passage and answer the question below.

   'However dramatic the rise of ministers, privy council and secretaries, Tudor government remained focused on the monarch. He took the final decision in great matters of state: war and peace, dynastic alliances, religious policy. Whether or not susceptible to influence, he took all the significant decisions in matters of patronage.'

   (Adapted from S.Gunn, *Early Tudor Government, 1485–1558*, Macmillan, 1995)

   How far do you agree with Gunn's assessment that Tudor government remained focused on the monarch?

2. 'The best servant I ever had'. Which of Henry's ministers does this best describe?

Henry VIII: an assessment

Religion: The religious situation at the end of Henry's reign was confused because the certainties of the old Catholic Church had been destroyed. There were still some Catholic practices in place, but other Catholic beliefs had been suppressed. Protestantism was a minority religion, with support confined to a few areas, largely in the south and east. However, the political settlement that emerged on Henry's death ensured that, at least in the short term, Protestantism would triumph. Despite the changes, England had avoided the religious wars that would characterise much of Western Europe as a distinctly national Church was established.

Foreign policy: Judged against his own aims, Henry's foreign policy can be judged a success. He had fulfilled his ambition as a military leader and warrior king. This was a considerable achievement as England lacked the resources to be a major military power and was often excluded or had to follow a reactive foreign policy. However, territorially his policies had brought little gain and this had also been at great cost. Although the country was never invaded, there were times when security was threatened.

Government: Henry's reign saw major changes in the way England was governed, particularly during the 1530s. Although two ministers dominated his reign, it does not mean that the King's role can or should be ignored. He intervened on many occasions to dramatic effect, deciding policy and making or breaking individuals. Faction was present throughout the reign and had an influence on policy, but it did not dominate the King. When ministers – or wives – failed the King, they were removed.

Henry's legacy: Although popular history remembers Henry as the King who had six wives, he made many changes to government, church and the monarchy that are still with us today. The last decade of his rule, which saw little benefit for the nation, should not overshadow the changes of the 1530s. The establishment of the Royal Supremacy and the Dissolution of the Monasteries were huge changes that should not be ignored. Parliament increased its role and statute law took on a greater significance, as the King-in-Parliament became supreme. His reign and that of his daughter, Elizabeth, are seen in contrast to the rule of his other two children, Edward and Mary, whose legacy was the Mid-Tudor Crisis. However, perhaps the most lasting legacy is the image of Henry as a colossus who had raised the status of the monarchy and bolstered national pride, to the extent that it was able to survive intact the subsequent rules of a minor and a woman.

Further reading

Texts specifically designed for students

Doran, S. *England and Europe 1485–1603* (Longman 1986)
Newcombe, D.G. *Henry VIII and the English Reformation* (Routledge 1995)
Randell, K. *Henry VIII and the Reformation in England* (Hodder)
Randell, K. *Henry VIII and the Government of England* (Hodder)

Texts for more advanced study

Duffy, E. *The Stripping of the Altars* (Yale, 1992) is a revisionist study of the Church on the eve of, and during, the Reformation, showing that traditional practices survived for a long time.

Duffy, E. *The Voices of Morebath* (Yale, 2001) is a study of a village in Devon showing how slow the progress of religious change was.

Elton, G. *Tudor Revolution in Government* (Cambridge University Press, 1953) is a work central to our understanding of changes in government in the 1530s and the contribution of Thomas Cromwell.

Haigh, C. *English Reformations: Religion, Politics and Society under the Tudors* (Oxford University Press, 1993) is a revisionist study of the Reformation.

MacCulloch, D. (ed) *The Reign of Henry VIII: Politics, Policy and Piety* (Macmillan, 1995) contains a series of essays on particular aspects of the reign.

MacCulloch, D. *Thomas Cranmer* (Yale, 1996) provides a detailed biography of the Archbishop who was at the centre of many of the changes, but whose role is often forgotten.

Scarisbrick, J. *Henry VIII* (Methuen, 1968), although detailed, remains the classic biography of Henry.

Starkey, D. *Six Wives, The Queens of Henry VIII* (Chatto and Windus, 2003) is a detailed study of Henry's reign and his relationship with his wives, superbly written and easy to read.

Starkey, D. *The Reign of Henry VIII: Personalities and Politics* (George Philip, 1985) is an excellent short study of Henry and the politics of his reign.

Wernham, R.B., *Before the Armada: the Growth of English Foreign Policy 1485–1558* (Cape 1966), is a detailed study of foreign policy throughout the period.

Index